THE SONGS OF
BOB DYLAN

THE SONGS OF

BOB DYLAN

FROM 1966 THROUGH 1975

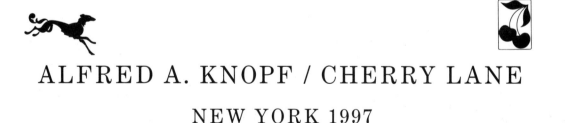

ALFRED A. KNOPF / CHERRY LANE

NEW YORK 1997

THIS IS A BORZOI BOOK

PUBLISHED BY ALFRED A. KNOPF, INC.

AND CHERRY LANE MUSIC CO., INC.

Published in the United States by Alfred A. Knopf, Inc., New York,
and simultaneously in Canada by Random House of Canada Limited, Toronto.
Distributed by Random House, Inc. New York.
Distributed to the music trade by Cherry Lane Music Co., Inc.
Greenwich, Connecticut 06830.

LIBRARY OF CONGRESS CATALOGING IN PUBLICATION DATA
Dylan, Bob
The songs of Bob Dylan
Includes index.
1. Music, Popular (Songs, etc.)—United States.
[M1630.18.D94B3 1978] 784
ISBN 0-394-73523-4 LC 77-18965 Paperback
ISBN 0-394-40888-8 LC 76-13692 Hardcover
Manufactured in the United States of America
Published November 15, 1976
Second Printing, March 1979
First Paperback Edition, September 1978
Reprinted Ten Times
Twelfth Printing, October 1997

*All of the songs in this book were arranged by Ronnie Ball
except for the following, which were arranged by Milton Okun:*

Odds and Ends
Million Dollar Bash
Goin' to Acapulco
Apple Suckling Tree
Lo and Behold!
Please, Mrs. Henry
Tears of Rage
Clothes Line Saga
Yea! Heavy and a Bottle of Bread
Tiny Montgomery
Crash on the Levee (Down in the Flood)
You Ain't Goin' Nowhere
Too Much of Nothing

This Wheel's on Fire
Open the Door, Homer
Long-Distance Operator
Nothing Was Delivered
Don't Ya Tell Henry
Hurricane
Mozambique
Black Diamond Bay
One More Cup of Coffee
Oh, Sister
Isis
Joey
Sara

Contents

*Most of these arrangements are in the same key as the original Bob Dylan recordings;
in a few cases the key has been changed to make it easier for the guitarist and pianist.*

THE SONGS OF
BOB DYLAN

I Want You

WORDS AND MUSIC BY
BOB DYLAN

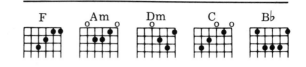

Moderately bright

Verse:

1. The

guilt - y un - der - tak - er sighs,___ The lone - some or - gan
drunk - en pol - i - ti - cian leaps___ Up - on the street___ where

grind - er cries,___ The sil - ver sax - o - phones___ say I___ should
moth - ers weep___ And the sav - iors who are fast___ a - sleep,___ They

re - fuse you.___ The cracked bells and
wait for you.___ And I wait for them to

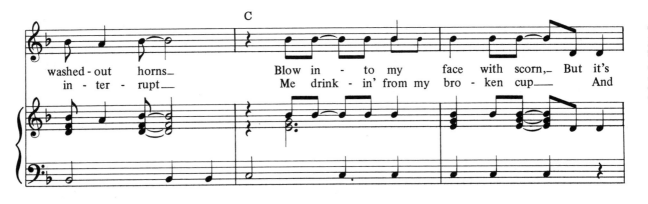

washed - out horns___
inter - rupt___

Blow in - to my face with scorn,_ But it's
Me drink - in' from my bro - ken cup___ And

not that way, I was-n't born___ to lose you.___
ask me___ to o - pen up___ the gate for you.___

Chorus:

I want you, I want you, I

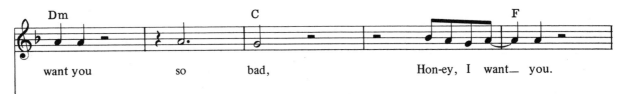

want you so bad, Hon-ey, I want_ you.

1. | 2. *To Interlude* | *Fine*

2. The Now

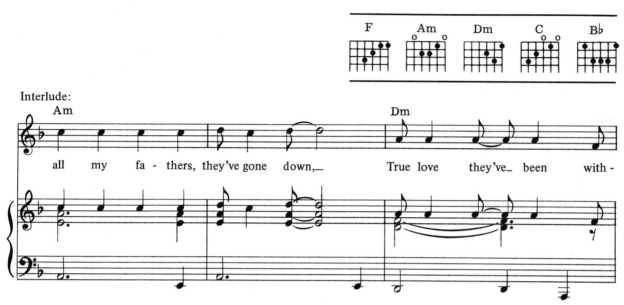

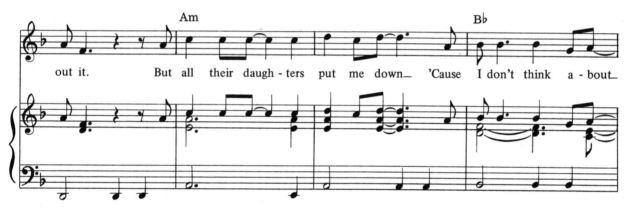

3.
F
Well, I return to the Queen of Spades
  | Am
And talk with my chambermaid.
Dm
She knows that I'm not afraid
  | C
To look at her.
Bb
She is good to me
C
And there's nothing she doesn't see.
  | Dm
She knows where I'd like to be
C
But it doesn't matter.
 | F | | Am
I want you, I want you,
 | Dm | | C
I want you so bad,
   | F
Honey, I want you.

4.
F
Now your dancing child with his Chinese suit,
  | Am
He spoke to me, I took his flute.
Dm
No, I wasn't very cute to him,
C
Was I?
  | Bb
But I did it, though, because he lied
C
Because he took you for a ride
  | Dm
And because time was on his side
  | C
And because I . . .
 | F | | Am
I want you, I want you,
 | Dm | | C
I want you so bad,
   | F
Honey, I want you.

Just Like a Woman

WORDS AND MUSIC BY

BOB DYLAN

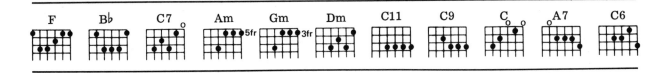

Visions of Johanna

WORDS AND MUSIC BY
BOB DYLAN

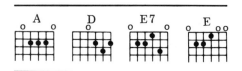

Moderately slow

1. Ain't it just like the night to play tricks when you're try-in' to be so
lot where the la - dies play blind - man's bluff with the
lit - tle boy lost, he takes him - self so se - ri - ous-
side the mu - se - ums, In - fin-i - ty goes up on

qui - et? We sit here strand-ed, though we're all
key chain And the all - night girls, they whis-
ly He brags of his mis-er - y, he likes
tri - al Voic-es ech - o this is what sal -

do-in' our best to de - ny it And Lou-
per of es - ca-pades out on the "D" train We can
to live dan - ger-ous-ly And when
va-tion must be like af - ter a while But Mo - na

VISIONS OF JOHANNA

2. In the emp-ty
3. Now,
4. In -
5. The ped-dler now speaks to the

count-ess who's pre-tend-ing to care for him_ Say-in',

"Name me some-one that's not a par-a-site and I'll_ go out_ and say_ a prayer_

____ for him." But like Lou-ise_ al-ways says,_ "Ya can't

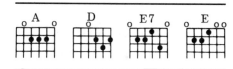

Stuck Inside of Mobile with the Memphis Blues Again

WORDS AND MUSIC BY
BOB DYLAN

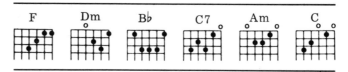

deep in - side_ my heart ____ I know I ___ can't es - cape. ___

Oh, Ma - ma, ____ can this real - ly be __ the end, ___ To be stuck_

__ in - side_ of Mo - bile With the Mem-phis blues_ a - gain. _____ 2. Well,

F　　Dm　　Bb　　C7　　Am　　C

2.

F　　　　　　|Dm
Well, Shakespeare, he's in the alley
|F　　　　　　|Dm　　|
With his pointed shoes and his bells,
F　　　　　|Dm
Speaking to some French girl,
|Bb　　　　|C7
Who says she knows me well.
|Bb　　　|F
And I would send a message
|Dm　　　|F
To find out if she's talked,
|Dm　　　　　|F
But the post office has been stolen
|Bb　　|F　　　|
And the mailbox is locked.
Am|　　　　|　　　　　|
Oh, Mama, can this really be the end,
|F　　　C　　|Dm
To be stuck inside of Mobile
F　　|Bb　　　　|F　　　|　　||
With the Memphis blues again.

3.

F　　　　　　|Dm
Mona tried to tell me
|F　　　　　　|Dm
To stay away from the train line.
|F　　　　　|Dm
She said that all the railroad men
|Bb　　　　　　|C7
Just drink up your blood like wine.
|Bb　　　　|F
An' I said, "Oh, I didn't know that,
|Dm　　　　　　|F
But then again, there's only one I've met
|Dm　　　　|F
An' he just smoked my eyelids
|Bb　　　　　　　　|F　　|
An' punched my cigarette."
Am|　　　　|　　　　　|
Oh, Mama, can this really be the end,
|F　　　C　　|Dm
To be stuck inside of Mobile
F　　|Bb　　　　|F　　|　　||
With the Memphis blues again.

4.

F　　　　　　　|Dm
Grandpa died last week
|F　　　　　|Dm
And now he's buried in the rocks,
|F　　　　　|Dm
But everybody still talks about
|Bb　　　|C7
How badly they were shocked.
|Bb　　　|F
But me, I expected it to happen,
|Dm　　|F
I knew he'd lost control
|Dm　　|F
When he built a fire on Main Street
|Bb　　|F　　|
And shot it full of holes.
Am|　　　　|　　　　|
Oh, Mama, can this really be the end,
|F　　C　　|Dm
To be stuck inside of Mobile
F　　|Bb　　|F　　　|　　||
With the Memphis blues again.

5.

F　　　·　|Dm
Now the senator came down here
|F　　　|Dm　　|
Showing ev'ryone his gun,
F　　　|Dm
Handing out free tickets
|Bb　　　|C7
To the wedding of his son.
|Bb　　　|F
An' me, I nearly got busted
|Dm　　　|F
An' wouldn't it be my luck
|Dm　　　|F
To get caught without a ticket
|Bb　　　|F　　|
And be discovered beneath a truck.
Am|　　　|　　　|
Oh, Mama, can this really be the end,
|F　　C　|Dm
To be stuck inside of Mobile
F　|Bb　　|F　　|　||
With the Memphis blues again.

6.

F　　　　|Dm
Now the preacher looked so baffled
|F　　　|Dm
When I asked him why he dressed
|F　　　|Dm　|
With twenty pounds of headlines
Bb　　|C7
Stapled to his chest.
|Bb　　|F
But he cursed me when I proved it to him,
|Dm　　|F
Then I whispered, "Not even you can hide.
|Dm　|F
You see, you're just like me,
|Bb　|F　　|
I hope you're satisfied."
Am|　　|　　　|
Oh, Mama, can this really be the end,
|F　C　|Dm
To be stuck inside of Mobile
F　|Bb　　|F　　|　||
With the Memphis blues again.

7.

F　　　　　|Dm
Now the rainman gave me two cures,
|F　　　|Dm
Then he said, "Jump right in."
|F　　|Dm
The one was Texas medicine,
|Bb　　|C7
The other was just railroad gin.
|Bb　　|F
An' like a fool I mixed them
|Dm　　|F
An' it strangled up my mind,
|Dm　|F
An' now people just get uglier
|Bb　|F　　|
An' I have no sense of time.
Am|　　|　　　|
Oh, Mama, can this really be the end,
|F　C　|Dm
To be stuck inside of Mobile
F　|Bb　　|F　　|　||
With the Memphis blues again.

8.

F　　　　　|Dm
When Ruthie says come see her
|F　　　|Dm
In her honky-tonk lagoon,
|F　　　|Dm
Where I can watch her waltz for free
|Bb　　|C7
'Neath her Panamanian moon.
|Bb　　|F
An' I say, "Aw come on now,
|Dm　　|F
You must know about my debutante."
|Dm　　　　|F
An' she says, "Your debutante just knows what you need
|Bb　|F　　|
But I know what you want."
Am|　　|　　|
Oh, Mama, can this really be the end,
|F　C　|Dm
To be stuck inside of Mobile
F　|Bb　|F　　|　||
With the Memphis blues again.

9.

F　　　　|Dm
Now the bricks lay on Grand Street
|F　　|Dm
Where the neon madmen climb.
|F　　|Dm
They all fall there so perfectly,
|Bb　　|C7
It all seems so well timed.
|Bb　|F
An' here I sit so patiently
Dm　　|F
Waiting to find out what price
|Dm　　|
You have to pay to get out of
F　　|Bb　|F　|
Going through all these things twice.
Am|　　|　　|
Oh, Mama, can this really be the end,
|F　C　|Dm
To be stuck inside of Mobile
F　|Bb　|F　　C|Dm　F|Bb　|F　||
With the Memphis blues again.

Rainy Day Women #12 & 35

WORDS AND MUSIC BY
BOB DYLAN

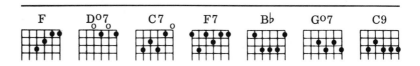

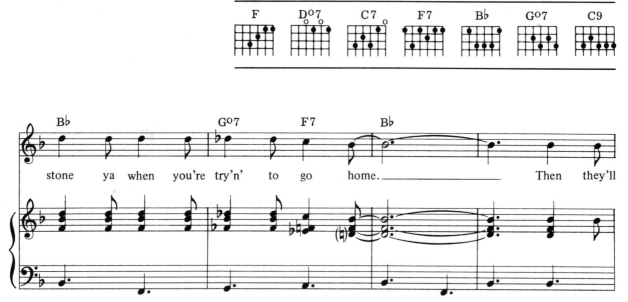

stone ya when you're try'n' to go home._____ Then they'll

stone ya when you're there all a - lone._____ But I

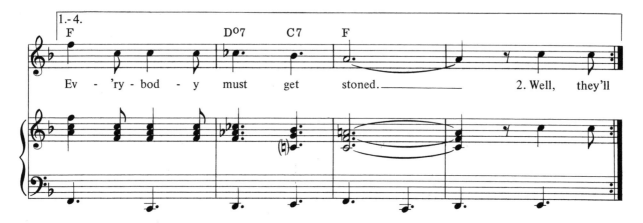

would not_____ feel_____ so all a - lone,_____

Ev - 'ry - bod - y must get stoned._____ 2. Well, they'll

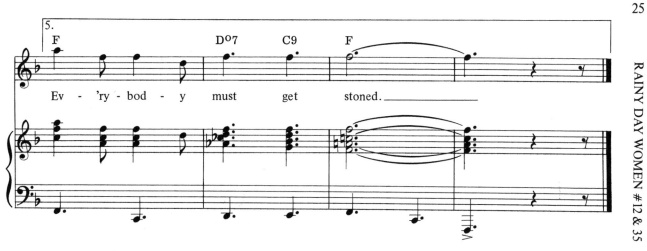

5.
F   D°7   C9   F

Ev - 'ry - bod - y   must   get   stoned._____

F | D°7   C7 | F |
2.   Well, they'll stone ya when you're walkin' 'long the street.
                 | | D°7   C7 | F | F
     They'll stone ya when you're tryin' to keep your seat.
     F7 | Bb | G°7   F7 | Bb |
     They'll stone ya when you're walkin' on the floor.
         | F | D°7   C7 | F | F
     They'll stone ya when you're walkin' to the door.
     F7 | C7 | | | |
     But I would not feel so all alone,
     F | D°7   C7| F | ||
     Everybody must get stoned.

           F | D°7   C7 | F |
3.   They'll stone ya when you're at the breakfast table.
                 | | D°7 C7 | F | F
     They'll stone ya when you are young and able.
     F7 | Bb | G°7   F7 | Bb |
     They'll stone ya when you're tryin' to make a buck.
         | F | D°7   C7 | F | F
     They'll stone ya and then they'll say, "Good luck."
     F7 | C7 | | | |
     Tell ya what, I would not feel so all alone,
     F | D°7   C7| F | ||
     Everybody must get stoned.

                  F | D°7 C7 | F |
4.   Well, they'll stone you and say that it's the end.
                    | | D°7   C7 | F | F
     Then they'll stone you and then they'll come back again.
     F7 | Bb | G°7   F7 | Bb |
     They'll stone you when you're riding in your car.
         | F | D°7   C7 | F | F
     They'll stone you when you're playing your guitar.
     F7 | C7 | | | |
     Yes, but I would not feel so all alone,
     F | D°7   C7| F | ||
     Everybody must get stoned.

                 F | D°7   C7| F |
5.   Well, they'll stone you when you walk all alone.
                  | | D°7 C7 | F | F
     They'll stone you when you are walking home.
     F7 | Bb | G°7 F7 | Bb |
     They'll stone you and then say you are brave.
         | F | D°7   C7 | F | F
     They'll stone you when you are set down in your grave.
     F7 | C7 | | | |
     But I would not feel so all alone,
     F | D°7   C7| F | ||
     Everybody must get stoned.

Temporary Like Achilles

WORDS AND MUSIC BY
BOB DYLAN

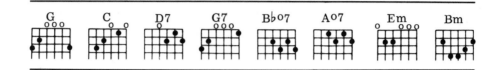

Moderately slow, with a feeling of $\frac{12}{8}$

1. Stand - ing on your win - dow, hon - ey, Yes, I've been here be - fore.
2. Kneel - ing 'neath your ceil - ing, Yes, I guess I'll be here for a while.
   rush in - to your hall - way, Lean a - gainst your vel - vet door.
   chil - les is in your al - ley - way, He don't want me here, He does brag.

I'm
I
He's

Feel - ing so harm - less, I'm look - ing at your sec - ond door.
tryin' to read your por - trait, but, I'm help - less, like a rich man's child.
watch up - on your scor - pion Who crawls a - cross your cir - cus floor.
point - ing to the sky And he's hun - gry like a man in drag.

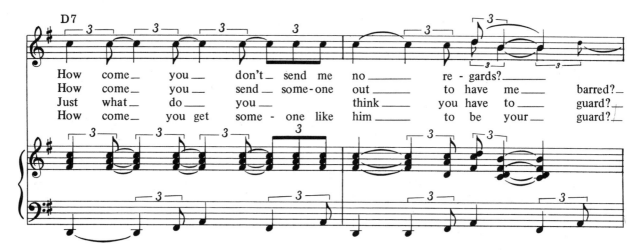

How come____ you____ don't____ send me___ no_____ re - gards?_____
How come____ you____ send____ some-one out_____ to have me____ barred?____
Just what____ do____ you_____ think_____ you have to____ guard?
How come____ you get some - one like him_____ to be your____ guard?

You
You
You
You

know I_____ want your lov - in',_____
know I_____ want your lov - in',_____
know I_____ want your lov - in',_____
know I_____ want your lov - in',_____

To Coda
(last time)

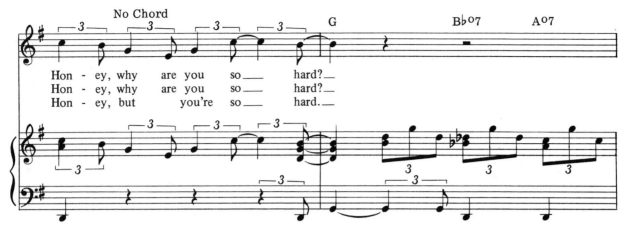

No Chord · G · B♭°7 · A°7

Hon - ey, why are you so ___ hard? ___
Hon - ey, why are you so ___ hard? ___
Hon - ey, but you're so ___ hard. ___

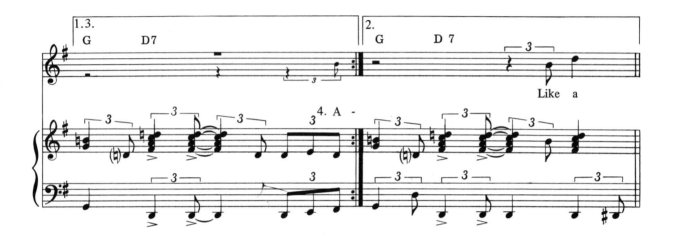

1.3. G D7 · 2. G D7

4. A -

Like a

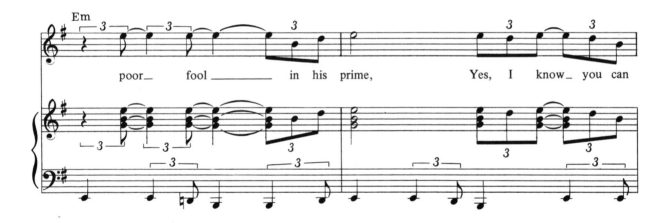

Em

poor ___ fool _____ in his prime, Yes, I know ___ you can

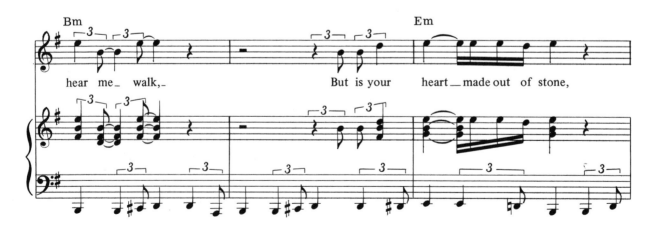

Bm · Em

hear me ___ walk, ___ But is your heart ___ made out of stone,

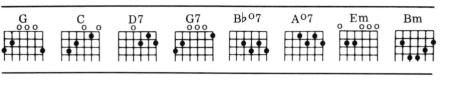

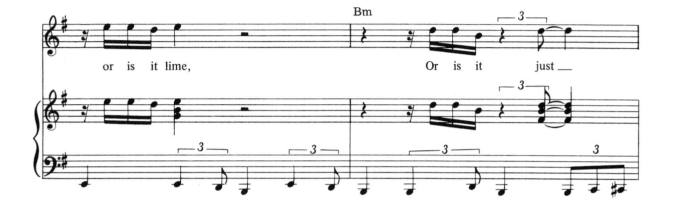

or is it lime,　　　Or is it just ___

D7　　　　　　　　　　　　　D. C. (with repeat) al Coda

sol - id ___ rock? ___　　　　3. Well, ___ I

Coda

N.C.　　　G　　Bb°7　A°7　　G　D7　G7

Hon - ey, but you're so ___ hard. ___

Absolutely Sweet Marie

WORDS AND MUSIC BY
BOB DYLAN

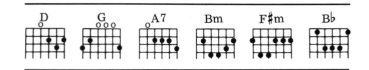

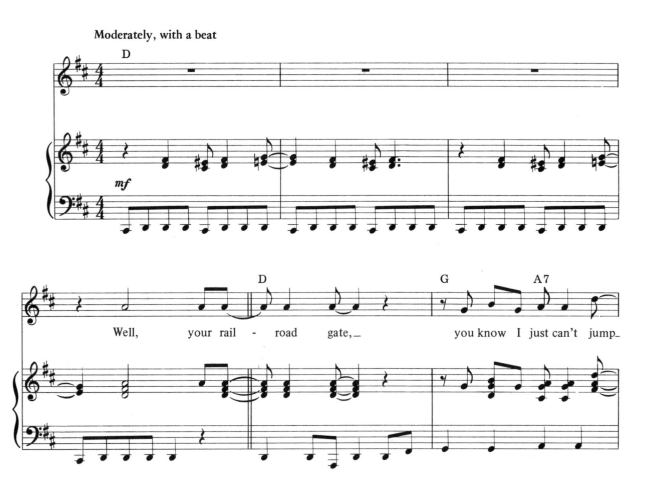

Well, your rail - road gate,— you know I just can't jump— it. Some-times it gets — so hard, you see.—

I'm just sit-ting here_ beat-ing on my trum-

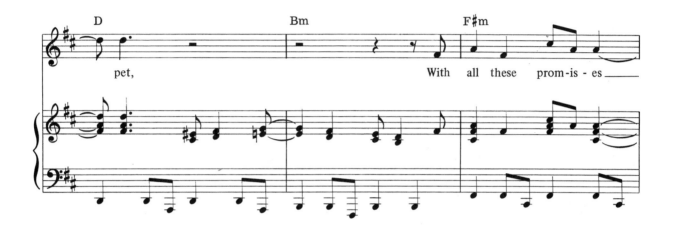

pet, With all these prom-is-es _____

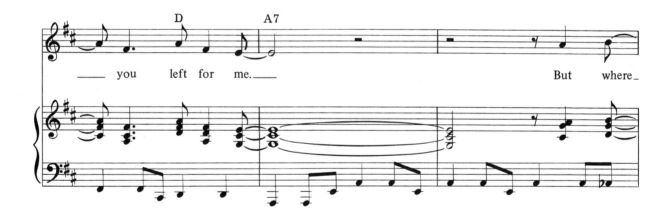

_____ you left for me._ But where_

_____ are you_ to-night,_ sweet Ma-rie?_ Well, I

wait - ed for you ___ when I was half ___ sick.
jail when all my mail ___ showed

Yes, I wait - ed for you ___ when you hat - ed
That a man can't give his ___ ad - dress out to bad com - pa -

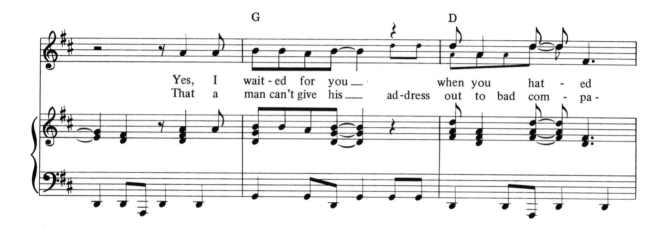

me. Well, ___ I wait - ed for you ___
ny, And now I stand here

in - side of the fro - zen traf - fic When you
look - in' at your yel - low rail - road In the

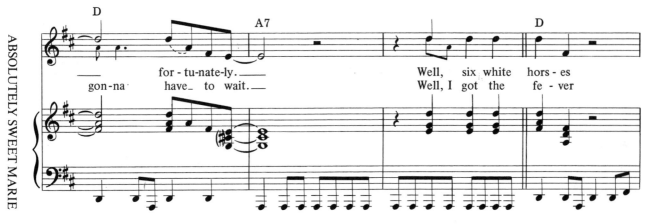

for - tu-nate-ly.____
gon-na have_ to wait.____
Well, six white hors - es
Well, I got the fe - ver

that you did prom - ise
down in my pock - ets,
Were fi-n'lly de - liv-ered down_
The Per-sian drunk-

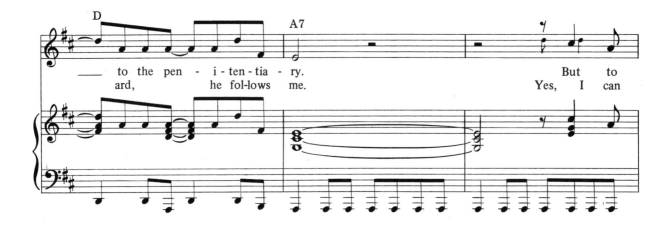

____ to the pen - i - ten-tia - ry.
ard, he fol-lows me.
But to
Yes, I can

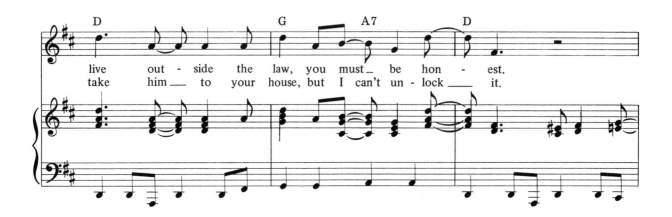

live out - side the law, you must_ be hon - est.
take him_ to your house, but I can't un - lock ____ it.

Obviously Five Believers

WORDS AND MUSIC BY

BOB DYLAN

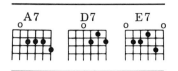

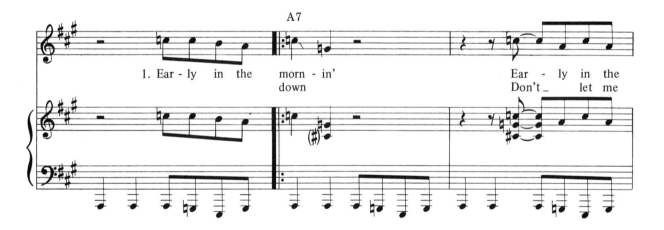

1. Ear - ly in the morn - in'
down

Ear - ly in the
Don't _ let me

morn - in'
down

I'm call - in' you _ to
I won't let you _ down

I'm call - in' you ___ to   Please come home ___
I won't let you ___ down   No I won't ___

A7

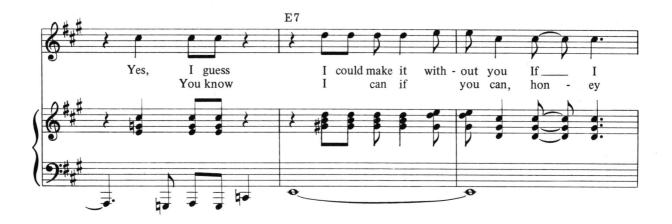

E7

Yes, I guess I could make it with - out you If ___ I
You know I can if you can, hon - ey

D7   No Chord   A7

just did - n't feel ___ so all a - lone.
But, hon - ey, please ___ don't.

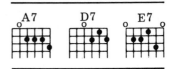

3.
   A7
I got my black dog barkin'

Black dog barkin'
|D7
Yes it is now

Yes it is now
|A7
Outside my yard
|E7
Yes, I could tell you what he means
D7 N.C. |A7
If I just didn't have to try so hard

4.
   A7
Your mama's workin'

Your mama's moanin'
|D7
She's cryin' you know

She's tryin' you know
|A7
You better go now
|E7
Well, I'd tell you what she wants
D7 N.C.| |A7
But I just don't know how

5.
   A7
Fifteen jugglers

Fifteen jugglers
|D7
Five believers

Five believers
|A7
All dressed like men
|E7
Tell yo' mama not to worry because
D7 N.C.| |A7
They're just my friends

6.
   A7
Early in the mornin'

Early in the mornin'
|D7
I'm callin' you to

I'm callin' you to
|A7
Please come home
|E7
Yes, I could make it without you
D7 N.C.| |A7
If I just did not feel so all alone

One of Us Must Know (Sooner or Later)

WORDS AND MUSIC BY
BOB DYLAN

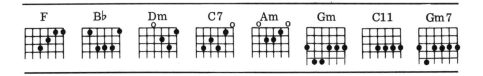

1. I did - n't mean _____ to treat you
   could - n't see _____ what you could
   could - n't see _____ when it start - ed

so bad _____ You should - n't take _ it so
show me _____ Your scarf had kept _ your
snow in' _____ Your voice was all _

per - son - al _____ I did - n't mean _____
mouth well hid _____ I could - n't see _____
that I heard _____ I could - n't see _____

to make you so sad _____
how you could know me _____ But you
where we were go - in' _____ But

You just hap - pened to be there, that's all ___
said you knew ___ me and I be - lieved you did ___
you said you knew an' I took your word ___ And

When I saw you say "good - bye" to your friend and smile
When you whis - pered in my ear
then you told me lat - er, as I a - pol - o - gized

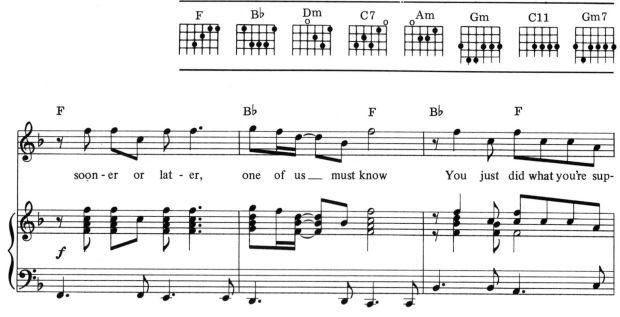

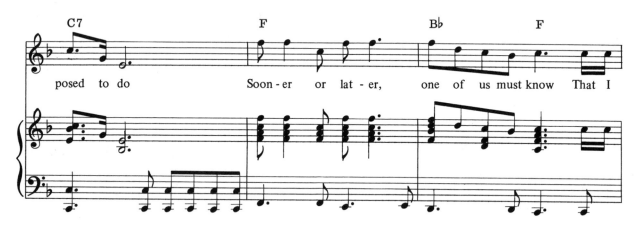

soon-er or lat-er, one of us _ must know You just did what you're sup-

posed to do Soon-er or lat-er, one of us must know That I

real-ly did_try to get close to you

2. I
3. I

Sad-Eyed Lady of the Lowlands

WORDS AND MUSIC BY
BOB DYLAN

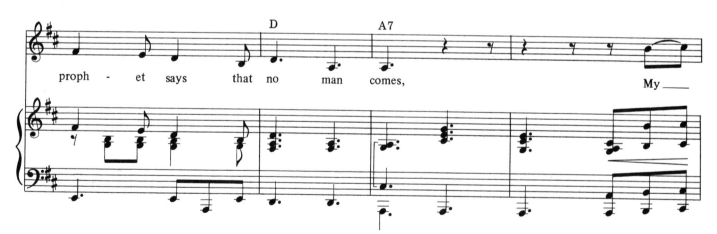

2.
```
    D           |A          |G        |Em7 A7
```
With your sheets like metal and your belt like lace,
```
     |D     |A          |G           |Em A7
```
And your deck of cards missing the jack and the ace,
```
     |G       |F#m           |Em7 A7 |D     |
```
And your basement clothes and your hollow face,
```
     |Em7                |Em7     A |Em A7
```
Who among them can think he could outguess you?
```
     |D         |A         |G        |Em7 A7|
```
With your silhouette when the sunlight dims
```
D        |A        |G        |Em A7
```
Into your eyes where the moonlight swims,
```
     |G      |F#m         |Em7 A7       |D     |
```
And your match-book songs and your gypsy hymns,
```
          |Em7|Em7       A        |Em A7     |
```
Who among them would try to impress you?
```
Em        |        |D        |A7      |Em
```
Sad-eyed lady of the lowlands,
```
                      |         |D     |A7        |
```
Where the sad-eyed prophet says that no man comes,
```
   |D  F#m|G     D|G     D|Em7 A7|A7        |
```
My warehouse eyes, my Arabian drums,
```
Em      |            |Em7 A |Em   A      |
```
Should I leave them by your gate,
```
     | Em      |         |D      A7|D      ||
```
Or, sad-eyed lady, should I wait?

3.
```
    D           |A          |G        |Em7 A7
```
The kings of Tyrus with their convict list
```
     |D      |A          |G        |Em A7
```
Are waiting in line for their geranium kiss,
```
     |G       |F#m           |Em7    A7|D        |
```
And you wouldn't know it would happen like this,
```
       |Em7            |Em7A     |Em A7
```
But who among them really wants just to kiss you?
```
     |D         |A         |G        |Em7 A7
```
With your childhood flames on your midnight rug,
```
     |D     |A        |G        |Em A7
```
And your Spanish manners and your mother's drugs,
```
     |G      |F#m         |Em7 A7|D     |
```
And your cowboy mouth and your curfew plugs,
```
           |Em7        |Em7  A      |Em A7   |
```
Who among them do you think could resist you?
```
Em      |        |D        |A7      |Em
```
Sad-eyed lady of the lowlands,
```
                      |         |D     |A7        |
```
Where the sad-eyed prophet says that no man comes,
```
   |D  F#m|G     D|G     D|Em A7|A7        |
```
My warehouse eyes, my Arabian drums,
```
Em      |            |Em7 A |Em   A
```
Should I leave them by your gate,
```
     | Em      |         |D      A7|D      ||
```
Or, sad-eyed lady, should I wait?

4.
```
    D           |A          |G        |Em A7
```
Oh, the farmers and the businessmen, they all did decide
```
     |D     |A          |G        |Em A7
```
To show you the dead angels that they used to hide.
```
         |G      |F#m         |Em7    A7    |D     |
```
But why did they pick you to sympathize with their side?
```
               |Em7           |Em7   A |Em A7
```
Oh, how could they ever mistake you?
```
     |D         |A         |G        |Em7 A7
```
They wished you'd accepted the blame for the farm,
```
         |D     |A        |G        |Em
```
But with the sea at your feet and the phony false alarm,
```
A7       |G      |F#m         |Em7 A7 |D        |
```
And with the child of a hoodlum wrapped up in your arms,
```
          |Em7        |Em7  A    |Em A7    |
```
How could they ever, ever persuade you?
```
Em      |        |D        |A7      |Em
```
Sad-eyed lady of the lowlands,
```
                      |         |D     |A7        |
```
Where the sad-eyed prophet says that no man comes,
```
   |D  F#m|G     D|G     D|Em7 A7|A7        |
```
My warehouse eyes, my Arabian drums,
```
Em      |            |Em7 A |Em   A
```
Should I leave them by your gate,
```
     | Em      |         |D      A7|D      ||
```
Or, sad-eyed lady, should I wait?

5.
```
    D           |A          |G        |Em7 A7
```
With your sheet-metal memory of Cannery Row,
```
     |D     |A          |G        |Em A7
```
And your magazine-husband who one day just had to go,
```
     |G       |F#m           |Em7       A7|D        |
```
And your gentleness now, which you just can't help but show,
```
     |Em7        |Em7    A      |Em7 A7
```
Who among them do you think would employ you?
```
     |D         |A         |G        |Em7 A7
```
Now you stand with your thief, you're on his parole
```
         |D  A         |G        |Em A7
```
With your holy medallion which your fingertips fold,
```
     |G      |F#m         |Em7       A7    |D     |
```
And your saintlike face and your ghostlike soul,
```
          |Em7        |Em7  A      |Em A7   |
```
Oh, who among them do you think could destroy you?
```
Em      |        |D        |A7      |Em
```
Sad-eyed lady of the lowlands,
```
                      |         |D     |A7        |
```
Where the sad-eyed prophet says that no man comes,
```
   |D  F#m|G     D|G     D|Em7 A7|A7        |
```
My warehouse eyes, my Arabian drums,
```
Em      |            |Em7 A |Em   A
```
Should I leave them by your gate,
```
     | Em      |         |D      A7|D      ||
```
Or, sad-eyed lady, should I wait?

Fourth Time Around

WORDS AND MUSIC BY
BOB DYLAN

Moderately

1. When she said, __ "Don't waste _____ your words, they're just __
2. I stood there __ and hummed, _____ I tapped on her __
3. She threw me __ out - side, _____ I stood in the __
4. Her Ja - mai - can rum _____ And when she did __
5. And when I __ was through, _____ I filled up my __

lies," _____ I cried __ she was deaf.
drum _____ and asked __ her how come.
dirt _____ where ev - 'ry - one walked.
come, _____ I asked __ her for some.
shoe _____ And brought __ it to you.

And she worked on __ my
And she but - toned __ her
And af - ter find - ing
She said, _____ "No,
And you, you took __ me

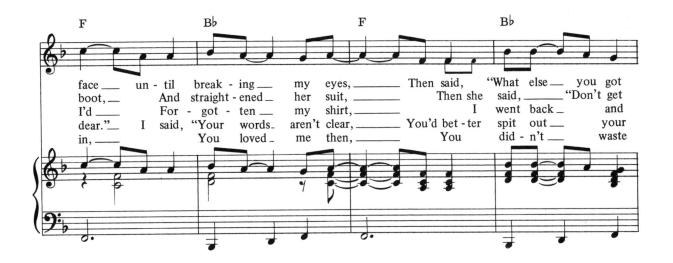

face __ un - til break - ing __ my eyes, _____ Then said, "What else __ you got
boot, __ And straight - ened __ her suit, _____ Then she said, _____ "Don't get
I'd __ For - got - ten __ my shirt, _____ I went back __ and
dear." I said, "Your words __ aren't clear, _____ You'd bet - ter spit out __ your
in, __ You loved __ me then, _____ You did - n't __ waste

To Coda ⊕

left?" It _____ was
cute." So _____ I
knocked. I _____
gum." She _____
time.

then that I ____ got up ____ to leave ____ But she ___ said, ___ "Don't___ for - get, ____
forced___ my ___ hands _____ in my pock - ets And ___ felt ___ with___ my thumbs,__
wait - ed in the hall - way, ___ she went to get ___ it, And I ___ tried ___ to ___ make sense, __
screamed ___ till her face got ___ so red, ___ Then she ___ fell ___ on ___ the floor, __

____ Ev - 'ry-
____ And
____ Out of that
____ And I

bod - y ___ must give some-thing back _____ For some - thing_ they get." __
gal - lant - ly hand - ed her My ___ ver - y ___ last piece_ of gum. __
pic - ture_ of you in your wheel - chair That_ leaned up ___ a - gainst. . .
cov - ered_ her up and then Thought_ I'd go ___ look through_ her drawer. __

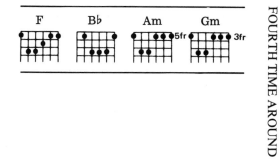

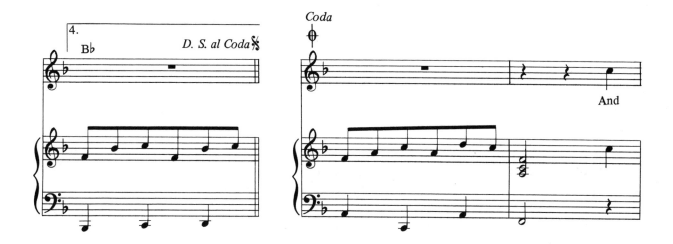

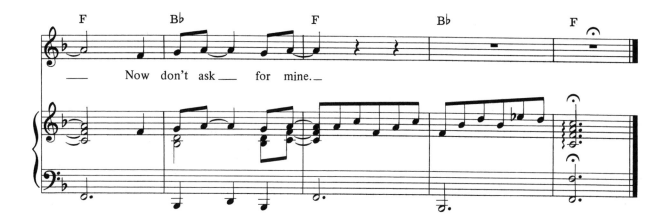

Most Likely You Go Your Way (and I'll Go Mine)

WORDS AND MUSIC BY

BOB DYLAN

Moderately, with a beat

You say you love me And you're thinkin' of me, But you
You say you disturb me And you don't deserve me, But you
You say you're sorry For tellin' stories That you

know you could be wrong.
know sometimes you lie.
know I believe are true.

I'll go last.— Then time will tell __ just who fell __ And
I'll go last.— Then time will tell __ just who fell __ And
I'll go last.— Then time will tell __ who fell __ And

who's been left be - hind,_____ When you go your way and I go
who's been left be - hind,_____ When you go your way and I go
who's been left be - hind,_____ When you go your way and I go

mine.
mine.

The judge, he holds a grudge,— He's gon-na call on you. __

Pledging My Time

WORDS AND MUSIC BY
BOB DYLAN

Slow Blues, with a feeling of 12/8

1. Well, ear-ly in the morn-

in'   'Til late at night,   I got a poi - son
ba - by?   I'll take you where you wan - na go.   And if it don't work
stuff-y,   I can hard - ly breathe.   Ev - 'ry-bod - y's gone but

head - ache,   But I feel all right.   I'm pledg - ing my
out,   You'll be the first to know.   I'm pledg - ing my
me and you   And I can't be the last to leave.   I'm pledg - ing my

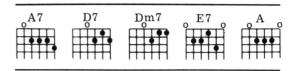

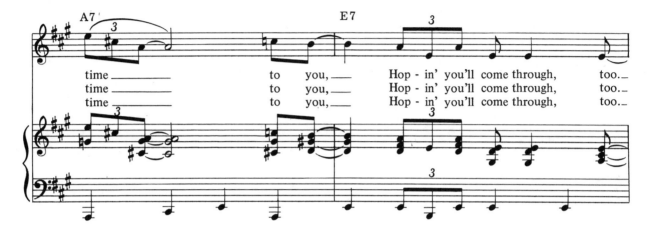

time _____ to you, ___ Hop - in' you'll come through, too._
time _____ to you, ___ Hop - in' you'll come through, too._
time _____ to you, ___ Hop - in' you'll come through, too._

2.Well, the ho - bo jumped_
4. (Instrumental)_____
6.Well, they sent for the ____

up, He came down nat - ur - 'lly. Af - ter he stole my ba-
am-bu-lance_ And one was sent. Some-bod - y got

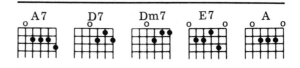

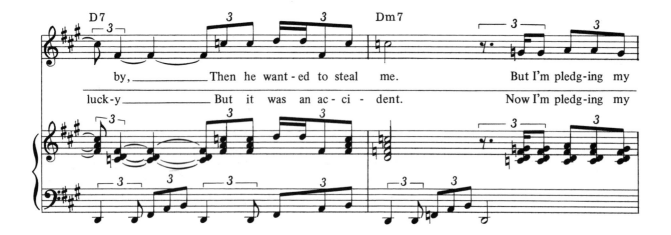

by, _____ Then he want-ed to steal me. But I'm pledg-ing my
luck-y _____ But it was an ac-ci - dent. Now I'm pledg-ing my

time to you, ____ Hop - in' you'll come through, too. __
time to you, ____ Hop - in' you'll come through, too. __

3. Won't you come with me,
5. Well, the room is so

Leopard-Skin Pill-Box Hat

WORDS AND MUSIC BY
BOB DYLAN

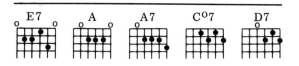

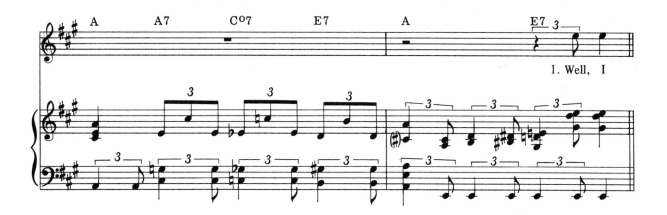

1. Well, I

see you got your___ brand new leop-ard-skin pill - box___ hat___

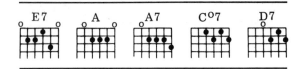

see you got your___ brand new leop - ard - skin pill - box ___ hat ___

tell me,___ ba - by, How your___ head ___ feels un - der some-thin' like ___ that

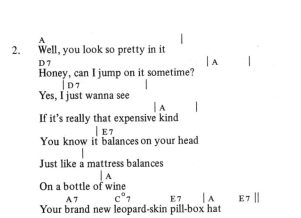

Un-der your brand new leop-ard-skin pill-box hat. ___ 2. Well, you ___

2.
A
Well, you look so pretty in it
D7 | A |
Honey, can I jump on it sometime?
| D7 |
Yes, I just wanna see
| A |
If it's really that expensive kind
| E7
You know it balances on your head
|
Just like a mattress balances
| A
On a bottle of wine
A7   C°7   E7 | A   E7 ||
Your brand new leopard-skin pill-box hat

3.
A
Well, if you wanna see the sun rise
D7 | A |
Honey, I know where
| D7 |
We'll go out and see it sometime
| A | |
We'll both just sit there and stare
E7
Me with my belt
'

Wrapped around my head
| |
And you just sittin' there
A   A7   C°7   E7 | A   E7 ||
In your brand new leopard-skin pill-box hat

4.
A
Well, I asked the doctor if I could see you
D7 | A |
It's bad for your health, he said
| D7
Yes, I disobeyed his orders
|
I came to see you
| A |
But I found him there instead
| E7
You know, I don't mind him cheatin' on me
| |
But I sure wish he'd take that off his head
A   A7   C°7   E7 | A   E7 ||
Your brand new leopard-skin pill-box hat

5.
A
Well, I see you got a new boyfriend
D7 | A |
You know, I never seen him before
| D7
Well, I saw him

Makin' love to you
| | A |
You forgot to close the garage door
| E7
You might think he loves you for your money
| |
But I know what he really loves you for
A   A7   C°7   E7 | A ||
It's your brand new leopard-skin pill-box hat

I'll Be Your Baby Tonight

WORDS AND MUSIC BY
BOB DYLAN

Moderately

Close your eyes, _____ close the door, _
_____ shut the shade, _

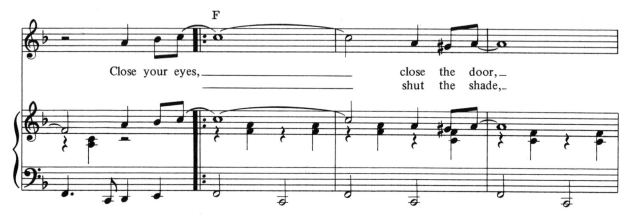

You don't have to wor-ry _____ an-y more. _
You don't have _____ to be a-fraid. _

I'll _____ be your
I'll _____ be your

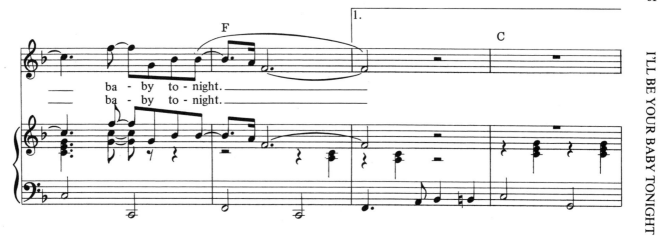

ba - by to - night.
ba - by to - night.

Shut the light,___ Well, that

mock - ing - bird's gon - na sail a - way,___ We're gon - na for -

get it. That big, fat moon___ is gon - na shine like a spoon,___ But,

we're gon - na let it, You won't re - gret it. Kick your shoes off, ___

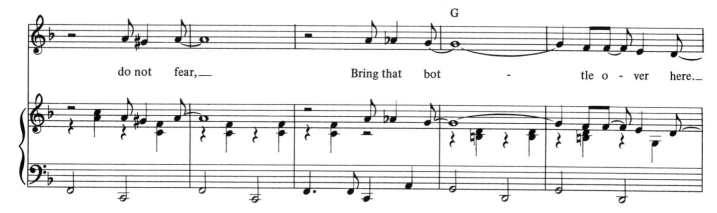

do not fear, ___ Bring that bot - tle o - ver here. ___

I'll ___ be your ___

___ ba - by to - night. ___

Dear Landlord

WORDS AND MUSIC BY
BOB DYLAN

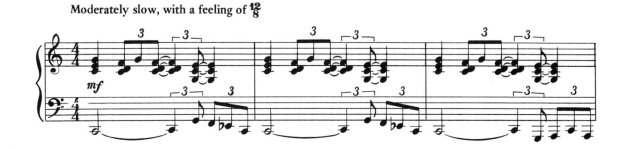

Moderately slow, with a feeling of $\frac{12}{8}$

Dear   land - lord,_
Dear   land - lord,_
Dear   land - lord,_

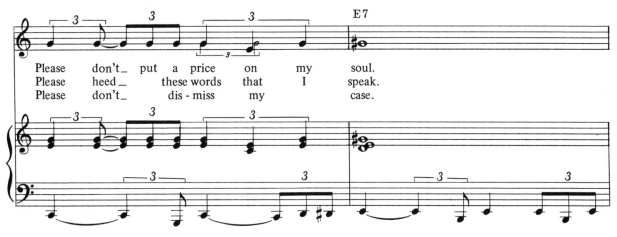

Please   don't_ put a price on my soul.
Please   heed_ these words that I speak.
Please   don't_ dis - miss my case.

My bur - den is heav - y, _____
I know you've suf - fered much, _____
I'm not a - bout to ar - gue, _____

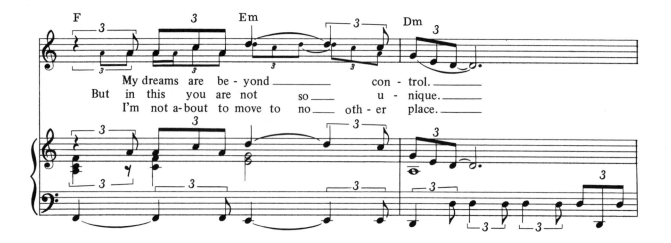

My dreams are be - yond _____ con - trol. _____
But in this you are not so _____ u - nique. _____
I'm not a - bout to move to no _____ oth - er place. _____

When that steam - boat whis - tle blows, _____
All of us, at times, we might
Now, each of us has his own

work too hard _____
spe - cial gift, _____
I'm gon - na give you all I _____ got to
To have it too fast and _____ too
And you know this was meant to _____ be

John Wesley Harding

WORDS AND MUSIC BY
BOB DYLAN

Moderately

John Wes - ley Har -
down in Chay - nee Coun -
All a - cross the tel -

ding — Was a friend — to — the poor, — He trav -
ty, — A time — they talk a - bout, — With his
e - graph His name — it did — re - sound, — But no —

'led with a gun — in ev - 'ry hand. —
la - dy by his side — He took a stand. —
— charge held a - gainst — him Could they prove. —

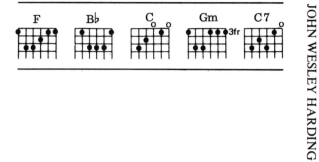

All a - long this coun-try - side,__ He
And soon the sit - u - a - tion there__ Was
And there was no man a - round__ Who could

o - pened a man-y a door, __ But he was nev - er known__ To
all but straight - ened out, __ For he was al - ways known__ To
track or chain him down, __ He was nev - er known__ To

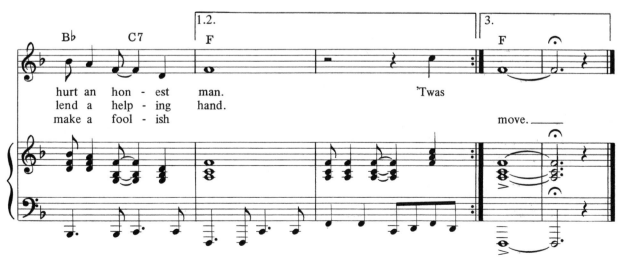

hurt an hon - est man. 'Twas
lend a help - ing hand.
make a fool - ish move. ___

As I Went Out One Morning

WORDS AND MUSIC BY
BOB DYLAN

I went out___ one morn - ing _____ To breathe the
part from me___ this mo ___ ment," _____ I
Just then___ Tom Paine,_ him - self,_ Came

air a - round_Tom Paine's,_ I spied the fair - est dam-
told her with_ my voice._ Said she, "But I don't wish_
run - ning from a-cross the field,_ Shout - ing at this love-

sel That ev - er did walk in chains._
___ to," Said I, "But you have no choice."_
ly girl_ And com-mand-ing her to yield._

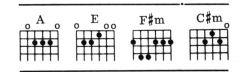

I of - fer'd her__ my hand, _____ She
"I beg__ you, sir,"__ she plead - ed _____ From the
And as she was let - ting go her grip,

took me by__ the arm.__ I knew__ that ver - y in -
cor - ners of __ her mouth,__ "I will se - cret - ly__ ac - cept__
Up Tom Paine__ did run, "I'm sor - ry, sir,"__ he said__

stant, ____ She meant __ to do me harm.__
__ you _____ And to - geth - er we'll fly south."
__ to me,_ "I'm sor - ry for what she's done."

"De -

I Dreamed I Saw St. Augustine

WORDS AND MUSIC BY
BOB DYLAN

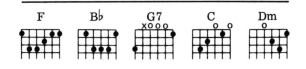

Slowly

1. I dreamed I saw St. Au - gus - tine,

A - live as you or me, Tear - ing through these

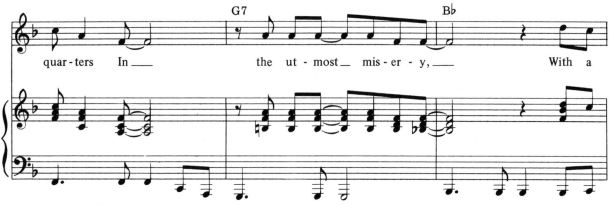

quar - ters In the ut - most mis - er - y, With a

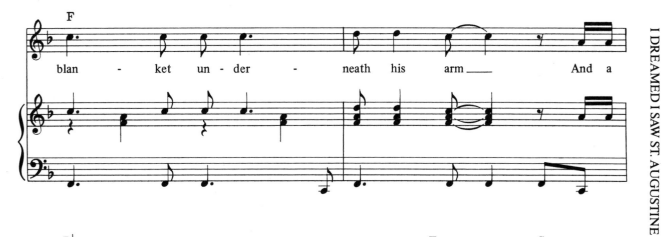

blan - ket un - der - neath his arm ____ And a

coat of sol - id gold, ____ Search-ing for ____ the

ver - y souls ____ Who al - read - y have ____ been sold. ____

2. "Arise, arise," he cried so loud,
   In a voice without restraint,
   "Come out, ye gifted kings and queens
   And hear my sad complaint.
   No martyr is among ye now
   Who you can call your own,
   So go on your way accordingly
   But know you're not alone."

3. I dreamed I saw St. Augustine,
   Alive with fiery breath,
   And I dreamed I was amongst the ones
   That put him out to death.
   Oh, I awoke in anger,
   So alone and terrified,
   I put my fingers against the glass
   And bowed my head and cried.

All Along the Watchtower

WORDS AND MUSIC BY
BOB DYLAN

Moderately, with a beat

"There must be some way out of here," said the jok-er to the thief,_

"There's too much _ con - fu - sion,

I can't get no re - lief._ Busi-ness-men,_ they

drink my wine,_ plow-men_ dig my earth, None of them a - long_

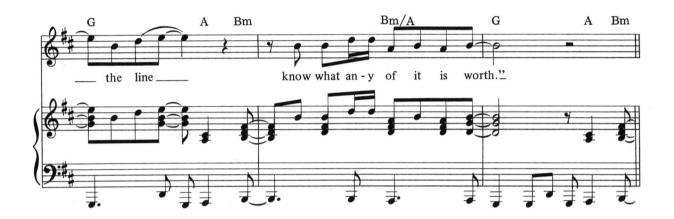

_ the line_ know what an-y of it is worth."

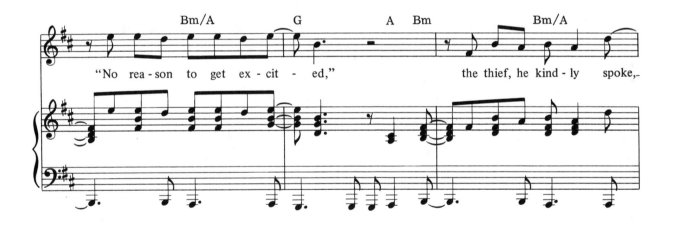

"No rea-son to get ex-cit-ed," the thief, he kind-ly spoke,_

"There are man-y here a-mong us_

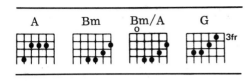

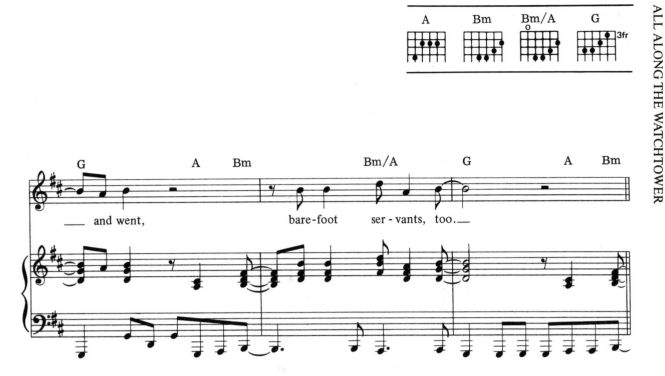

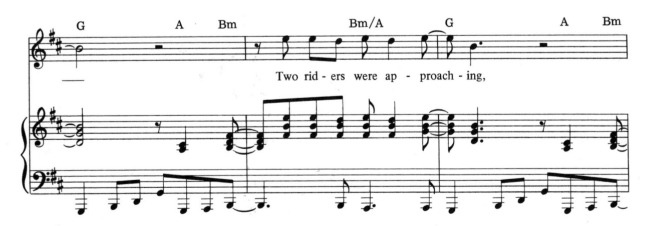

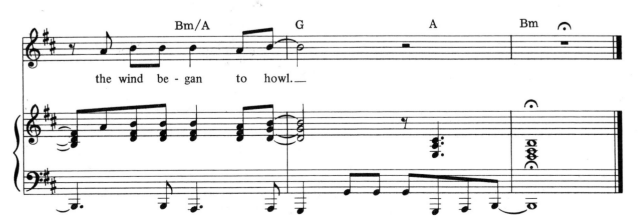

The Ballad of Frankie Lee and Judas Priest

WORDS AND MUSIC BY
BOB DYLAN

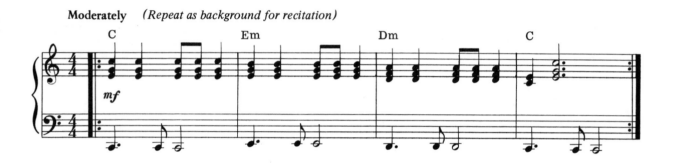

Moderately *(Repeat as background for recitation)*

1.
```
 C              | E m
Well, Frankie Lee and Judas Priest,
 | D m           | C
They were the best of friends.
 |                    | E m
So when Frankie Lee needed money one day,
 | D m             | C
Judas quickly pulled out a roll of tens
 |                | E m
And placed them on a footstool
 | D m          | C
Just above the plotted plain,
 |                   | E m
Sayin', "Take your pick, Frankie Boy,
 | D m          | C        ||
My loss will be your gain."
```

2.
```
 C               | E m
Well, Frankie Lee, he sat right down
 | D m          | C
And put his fingers to his chin,
 |                | E m
But with the cold eyes of Judas on him,
 | D m          | C
His head began to spin.
 |                              | E m
"Would ya please not stare at me like that," he said,
 | D m          | C
"It's just my foolish pride,
 |                    | E m
But sometimes a man must be alone
 | D m          | C        ||
And this is no place to hide."
```

3.
```
 C                   | E m
Well, Judas, he just winked and said,
 | D m                | C
"All right, I'll leave you here,
 |                    | E m
But you'd better hurry up and choose
                | D m
Which of those bills you want,
                | C        |
Before they all disappear."
                    | E m
"I'm gonna start my pickin' right now,
 | D m          | C        ||
Just tell me where you'll be."
```

4.
```
 C                   | E m
Judas pointed down the road
 | D m                | C      |
And said, "Eternity!"
                | E m
"Eternity?" said Frankie Lee,
 | D m          | C
With a voice as cold as ice.
 |                    | Em
"That's right," said Judas Priest, "Eternity,
 | D m                | C      ||
Though you might call it 'Paradise.'"
```

5.
```
 C              | E m        |
"I don't call it anything,"
 D m                | C      |
Said Frankie Lee with a smile.
                | E m
"All right," said Judas Priest,
 D m            | C        ||
"I'll see you after a while."
```

6.
 C | E m |
Well, Frankie Lee, he sat back down,
D m | C |
Feelin' low and mean,
     | E m |
When just then a passing stranger
D m | C
Burst upon the scene,
 | | E m
Saying, "Are you Frankie Lee, the gambler,
 | D m | C
Whose father is deceased?
 |
Well, if you are,
 | E m
There's a fellow callin' you down the road
 | D m | C ||
And they say his name is Priest."

7.
 C | E m
"Oh, yes, he is my friend,"
 | D m | C |
Said Frankie Lee in fright,
     | E m
"I do recall him very well,
 | D m | C |
In fact, he just left my sight."
      | E m
"Yes, that's the one," said the stranger,
 | D m | C
As quiet as a mouse,
 | | E m
"Well, my message is, he's down the road,
D m | C ||
Stranded in a house."

8.
 C | E m
Well, Frankie Lee, he panicked,
  | D m | C |
He dropped ev'rything and ran
     | E m
Until he came up to the spot
 | D m | C |
Where Judas Priest did stand.
     | E m
"What kind of house is this," he said,
 | D m | C
"Where I have come to roam?"
 | | E m
"It's not a house," said Judas Priest,
  | D m | C ||
"It's not a house . . . it's a home."

9.
 C | E m
Well, Frankie Lee, he trembled,
 | D m | C |
He soon lost all control
      | E m
Over ev'rything which he had made
  | D m | C
While the mission bells did toll.
 | |
He just stood there staring
Em | D m | C
At that big house as bright as any sun,
 | | E m
With four and twenty windows
 | D m | C ||
And a woman's face in ev'ry one.

10.
 C | E m
Well, up the stairs ran Frankie Lee
 | D m | C
With a soulful, bounding leap,
 | | E m
And, foaming at the mouth,
  | D m | C
He began to make his midnight creep.
 | | E m
For sixteen nights and days he raved,
  | D m | C |
But on the seventeenth he burst
     | E m
Into the arms of Judas Priest,
  | D m | C ||
Which is where he died of thirst.

11.
 C | E m
No one tried to say a thing
  | D m | C |
When they took him out in jest,
    | E m
Except, of course, the little neighbor boy
 | D m | C
Who carried him to rest.
 | | E m
And he just walked along, alone,
 | D m | C
With his guilt so well concealed,
    | E m |
And muttered underneath his breath,
D m | C ||
"Nothing is revealed."

12.
 C | E m
Well, the moral of the story,
 | D m | C
The moral of this song,
 | | E m
Is simply that one should never be
 | D m | C
Where one does not belong.
 | | E m |
So when you see your neighbor carryin' somethin',
D m | C
Help him with his load,
 | | E m
And don't go mistaking Paradise
 | D m | C ||
For that home across the road.

Drifter's Escape

WORDS AND MUSIC BY
BOB DYLAN

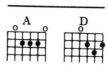

Moderately

"Oh, help me in my weak -
judge, he cast his robe ___
stop that curs - ed ju -

ness," I heard the drift - er say, ___
___ a - side, ___ A tear came to his eye, ___
ry," Cried the at - tend - ant and the nurse, ___

As they car - ried him ___ from the court-room And were tak -
"You fail to un-der - stand," he said, ___ "Why must ___
"The trial was bad e - nough, But this ___

ing him a - way. ___
___ you e - ven try?" "My trip ___
___ is ten times worse." Just then ___ Out -

has -n't been a pleas - ant one And my \
side, the crowd was stir - ring, You could \
a bolt of light - ning Struck the

time it is - n't long, And I \
hear it from the door. In - side, \
court-house out of shape, And while ev -

still do not know What it was that I've done wrong." \
the judge was step - ping down, While the ju - ry cried for more. \
'ry - bod - y knelt to pray The drift - er did es - cape.

1.2. \
Well, the \
"Oh,

3.

I Am a Lonesome Hobo

WORDS AND MUSIC BY
BOB DYLAN

1. I am ____ a lone - some ho - bo With - out fam - i - ly ____ or friends, Where an - oth - er man's ____ life might be - gin, ____ That's ex - act - ly where ____ mine

2.
G   C | G
Well, once I was rather prosperous,
C |G   C | G   C | G
There was nothing I did lack.
  C | G   C | G
I had fourteen-karat gold in my mouth
C | G   C | G
And silk upon my back.
    C | G   C | G
But I did not trust my brother,
C | G   C | G   C | G
I carried him to blame,
C | G   D | C   G
Which led me to my fatal doom,
 | C   D7 | G   C ||
To wander off in shame.

3.
G   C | G   c |
Kind ladies and kind gentlemen,
G   c | G   c | G
Soon I will be gone,
c | G   c | G   c |
But let me just warn you all,
G   c | G   c | G
Before I do pass on;
c | G   c | G   c |
Stay free from petty jealousies,
G   c | G   c | G
Live by no man's code,
C   G   D | C   G
And hold your judgment for yourself
 | C   D7 | G ||
Lest you wind up on this road.

The Wicked Messenger

WORDS AND MUSIC BY

BOB DYLAN

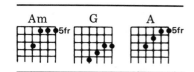

Moderately

1. There was a wick-ed mes-sen-ger___ From E-li he did come, With a mind that mul-ti-plied___ The small-est mat-ter. When ques-tioned who had sent for him, He an-swered with his

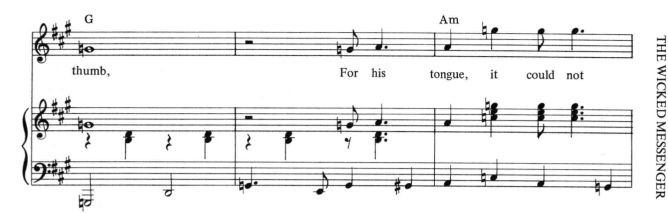

thumb, For his tongue, it could not

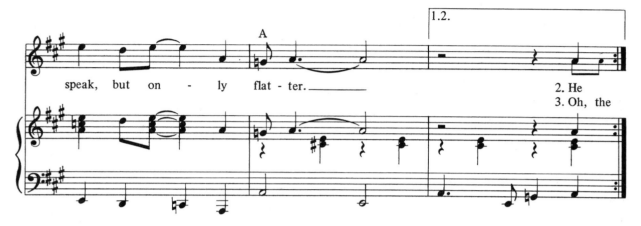

speak, but on - ly flat - ter. _____ 2. He
3. Oh, the

2. Am
   He stayed behind the assembly hall,
                    G
   It was there he made his bed,
   Am   A
   Oftentimes he could be seen returning.
      Am
   Until one day he just appeared
                    G
   With a note in his hand which read,
      Am   A
   "The soles of my feet, I swear they're burning."

3. Am
   Oh, the leaves began to fallin'
                    G
   And the seas began to part,
      Am   A
   And the people that confronted him were many,
      Am
   And he was told but these few words,
                    G
   Which opened up his heart,
      Am   A   Am   A
   "If ye cannot bring good news, then don't bring any."

Down Along the Cove

WORDS AND MUSIC BY
BOB DYLAN

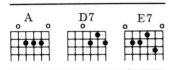

Medium beat

Down a-long the cove,
Down a-long the cove,
Down a-long the cove,

I spied my
I spied my
We walked to-

true love com-in' my way.
lit-tle bun-dle of joy.
geth-er hand in hand.

Down a-long the cove,
Down a-long the cove,
Down a-long the cove,

I spied my true
I spied my lit-
We walked to-geth-

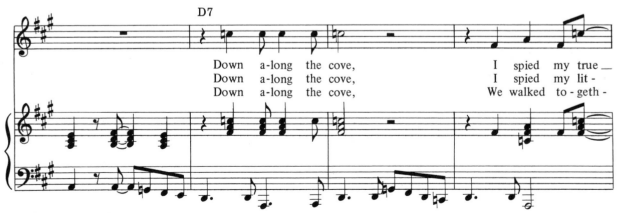

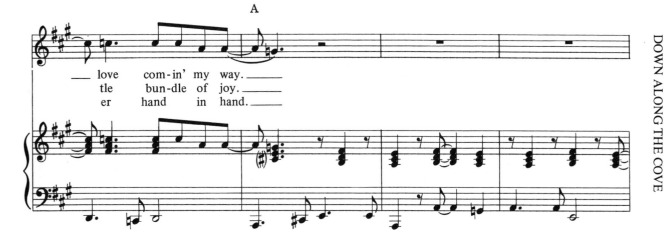

love com-in' my way. _____
tle bun-dle of joy. _____
er hand in hand. _____

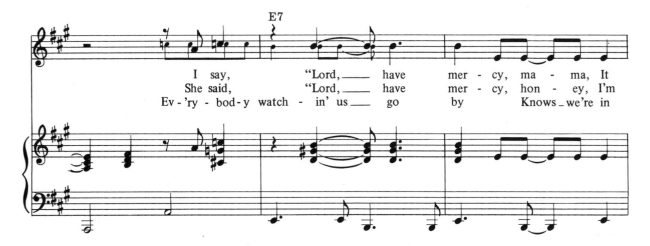

I say, "Lord, _____ have mer - cy, ma - ma, It
She said, "Lord, _____ have mer - cy, hon - ey, I'm
Ev -'ry - bod-y watch - in' us _____ go by Knows _ we're in

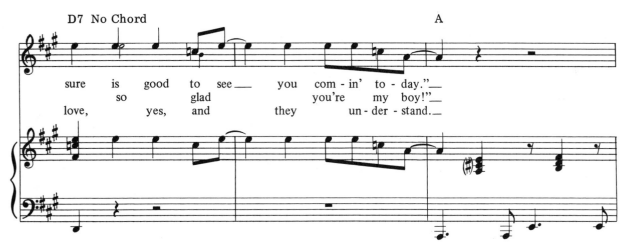

sure is good to see _____ you com - in' to - day." _____
so glad you're my boy!" _____
love, yes, and they un - der - stand. _____

I Pity the Poor Immigrant

WORDS AND MUSIC BY
BOB DYLAN

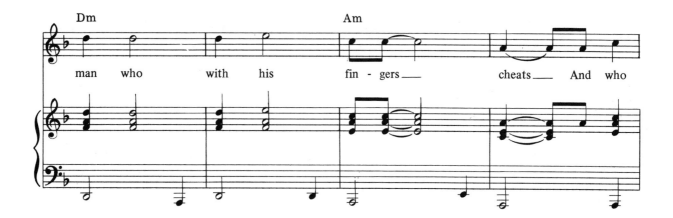

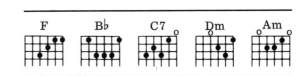

Who pas - sion - ate - ly hates his

life And like - wise, fears ___ his ___ death. ___

2. I pity the poor immigrant
   Whose strength is spent in vain,
   Whose heaven is like Ironsides,
   Whose tears are like rain,
   Who eats but is not satisfied,
   Who hears but does not see,
   Who falls in love with wealth itself
   And turns his back on me.

3. I pity the poor immigrant
   Who tramples through the mud,
   Who fills his mouth with laughing
   And who builds his town with blood,
   Whose visions in the final end
   Must shatter like the glass.
   I pity the poor immigrant
   When his gladness comes to pass.

Lay, Lady, Lay

WORDS AND MUSIC BY
BOB DYLAN

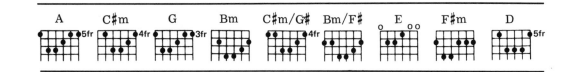

Slowly

Lay, la-dy, lay,_ lay a-cross my big brass bed _

Lay, la-dy, lay,_ lay a-cross my big brass bed _

What-ev-er col-ors you have_

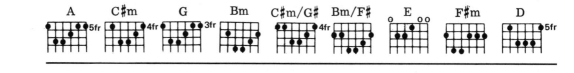

His clothes are dirt-y but his __ hands are clean_

And you're the best_ thing that he's ev-er seen_

Stay, la-dy, stay,_ stay with your man_ a-while

Why wait an-y long-er for __ the world to be-gin_

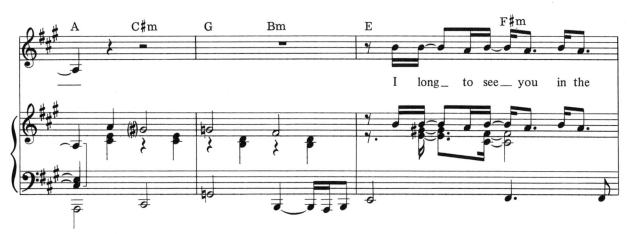

I long to see you in the morn-ing light_ I long to reach_for you in the night_

Stay, la-dy, stay,_ stay while the night_ is still a-head_

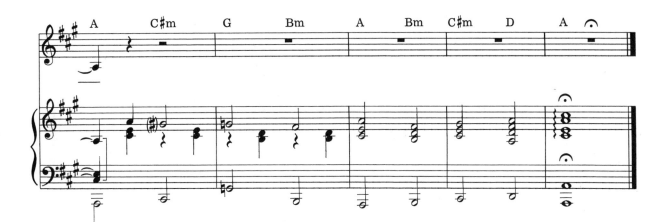

Nashville Skyline Rag

MUSIC BY
BOB DYLAN

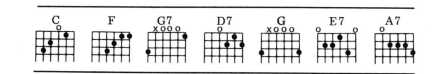

Bright Country style

Country Pie

WORDS AND MUSIC BY
BOB DYLAN

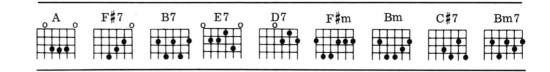

Moderately fast

Just like old Sax - o - phone Joe When he's got the hogs - head
up on his toe ___ Oh me, oh my ___
Love that coun - try pie ___ Lis - ten to the fid -

dler play   When he's play-in' 'til the break of day

Oh me, oh my____   Love that coun-try pie____

Rasp - ber - ry, straw-ber - ry, lem - on and lime__   What do I
don't need   much and that ain't   no lie __   Ain't run-nin' an - y

care?   Blue - ber - ry, ap - ple, cher - ry, pump-kin and plum__
race   Give to me my   coun - try pie __

Tell Me That It Isn't True

WORDS AND MUSIC BY
BOB DYLAN

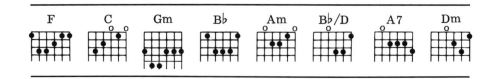

I have heard ru-mors all o-ver town,__ They say that you're plan - ning__ to put me down.__

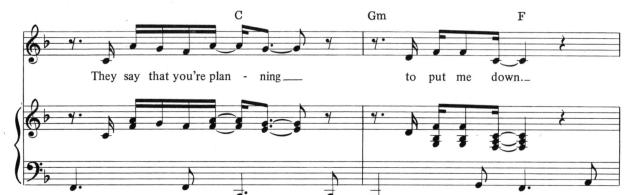

All I would like you to do,_____

Is tell me that it is-n't true. ___

They say ___ that you've been ___ seen

with some oth-er man, ___ That he's tall, dark and hand-some,

and you're hold-ing his hand. ___ Dar-lin', I'm a-count-in' on you, ___

Tell me that it is-n't true.___

To know___ that some oth - er man___ is

hold-in' you tight,___ It hurts me all o - ver,

it does-n't seem right._____

One More Night

WORDS AND MUSIC BY
BOB DYLAN

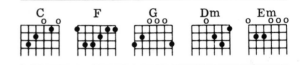

One   more   night,   the   stars   are _____   in
shame - ful   and   it's   sad,   I   lost   the   on - ly   pal _____   I
One   more   night,   I   will   wait   for _____   the

sight   But   to - night   I'm   as   lone - some   as   can
had,   I   just   could   not   be   what   she   want - ed   me   to
light   While   the   wind   blows   high   a - bove   the

be. _____
be. _____
tree. _____

Oh, the moon is shin - in'
I will turn my head up
Oh, I miss my dar - ling

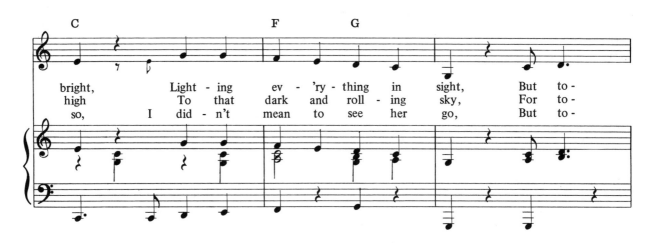

bright,   Light - ing   ev - 'ry - thing   in   sight,   But   to -
high   To   that   dark   and   roll - ing   sky,   For   to -
so,   I   did - n't   mean   to   see   her   go,   But   to -

To Coda | 1.

night   no __ light __ will shine on me.   Oh, it's
night   no __ light __ will shine on
night   no __ light __ will shine on

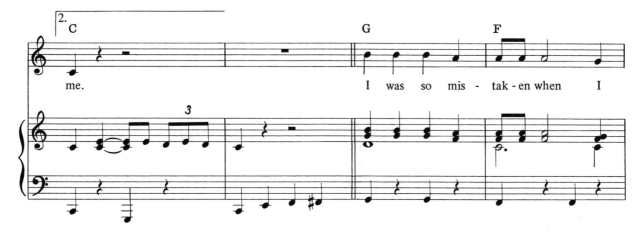

2.

me.   I was so mis - tak - en when   I

thought that she'd be true, I had no i - dea what _____ a

D. S. al Coda

wom - an in love would do.

Coda

me. One more night, the

moon is shin - in' bright And the wind blows high a - bove _ the

tree. _____ Oh, I miss that wom-an

so, _____ I did-n't mean to see her go, But to-

night no ___ light ___ will shine on me.

No Chord

Peggy Day

WORDS AND MUSIC BY
BOB DYLAN

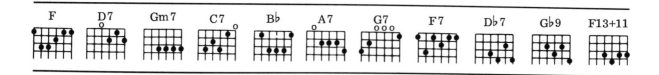

Peg - gy Day__ stole my poor heart a - way, ___
Peg - gy night__ makes my fu - ture look so bright,

By gol - ly, what more can I say, ___
Man, that girl ___ is out of sight,

Gm7　　　　C7　　　　1. F　　Bb　　F　C7

Love to spend the night with Peg - gy Day.
Love to spend the day with Peg - gy

2. F　　Bb　　F　　　　　　A7

night.　　　　Well, you know that e - ven be - fore I

D7

learned her name, You know I loved her___ just the same.___ An'

Gm7

I tell 'em all, wher - ev - er I may go,___ Just so they'll know, that

she's my lit - tle la - dy And I love ___ her so. ___

Peg - gy Day ___ stole my poor ___ heart a - way, Turned ___

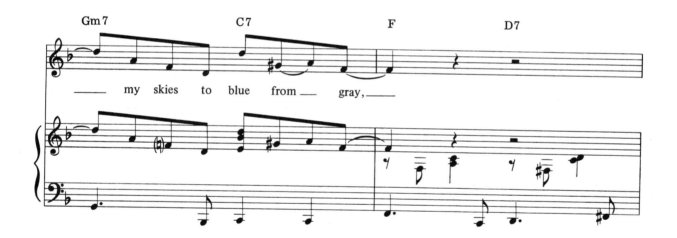

___ my skies to blue from ___ gray, ___

Love to spend the night with Peg - gy Day.

To Be Alone with You

WORDS AND MUSIC BY
BOB DYLAN

Moderately

To be a-lone with you,___ Just you and me,___

Now won't you tell me true,___

Ain't that the way it ought-a be? To hold each oth-er tight___

The whole night through,___ Ev-'ry-thing is al-ways right___

When I'm a - lone __ with you. __

To be a - lone with you __ At the close __ of the day __

With on-ly you in view __ While eve-ning __ slips a - way __

It on-ly goes to show __ That while life's pleas-ures be few, __

The on-ly one I know __ Is when I'm a-lone with you. __

They say that night-time is the right __ time To be __

__ with the one you love __ Too man-y thoughts get in the

way in the day __ But you're al-ways what I'm think-in' of __ I wish the night were here __

Bring-in' me all of your charms __

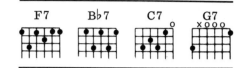

When on-ly you are near___ To hold me in your arms.___

___ I'll al-ways___ thank the Lord___

When my work-ing day's through___ I get my sweet re-ward___

___ To be a-lone with you.___

I Threw It All Away

WORDS AND MUSIC BY
BOB DYLAN

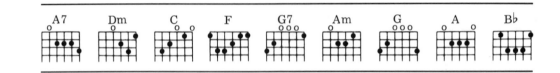

Slowly

I once held her_ in my arms,_ She said she would al-ways stay._

stay._ But I_ was cruel,_ I

makes the world go 'round,— Love and on - ly love,— it can't be de - nied.—

No mat - ter what you think a - bout— it

You just won't be a - ble to do with - out — it. Take a tip— from one who's tried.—

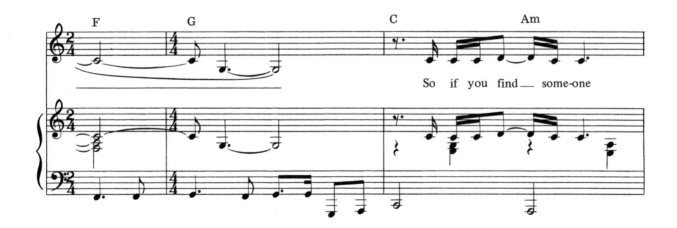

So if you find — some-one

Tonight I'll Be Staying Here with You

WORDS AND MUSIC BY
BOB DYLAN

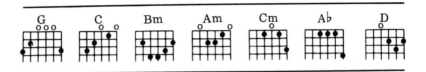

Throw my tick-et out the win - dow,

Throw my suit - case out there, too, ___ Throw my

trou - bles out the door, I don't need them an - y more 'Cause to-

night I'll be stay - ing here with you.

Throw my tick-et out __ the win-dow,

Throw my suit-case out __ there, too,

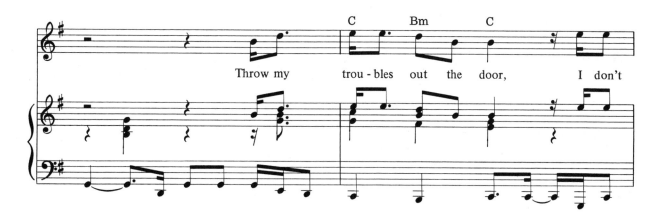

Throw my trou-bles out the door, I don't

need them an-y more 'Cause to-night I'll be stay-ing here with you.

Wanted Man

WORDS AND MUSIC BY
BOB DYLAN

Moderate Country style

1. Want-ed man ___ in Cal - i - for - nia, want-ed

man in Buf - fa - lo, ___ Want-ed man ___ in Kan - sas

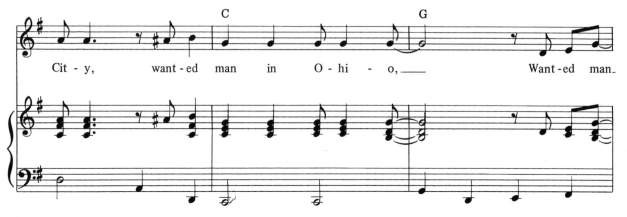

Cit - y, want-ed man in O - hi - o, ___ Want-ed man ___

in Mis - sis - sip - pi, want-ed man __ in old __ Chey - enne, __

Wher - ev - er you might look to - night, __ you might

see this want - ed man. __ 2. I might be __ __

2. I might be in Colorado or Georgia by the sea,
Working for some man who may not know at all who I might be.
If you ever see me comin' and if you know who I am,
Don't you breathe it to nobody 'cause you know I'm on the lam.

3. Wanted man by Lucy Watson, wanted man by Jeannie Brown,
Wanted man by Nellie Johnson, wanted man in this next town.
But I've had all that I've wanted of a lot of things I had
And a lot more than I needed of some things that turned out bad.

4. I got sidetracked in El Paso, stopped to get myself a map,
Went the wrong way into Juarez with Juanita on my lap.
Then I went to sleep in Shreveport, woke up in Abilene
Wonderin' why the hell I'm wanted at some town halfway between.

5. Wanted man in Albuquerque, wanted man in Syracuse,
Wanted man in Tallahassee, wanted man in Baton Rouge,
There's somebody set to grab me anywhere that I might be
And wherever you might look tonight, you might get a glimpse of me.

6. Wanted man in California, wanted man in Buffalo,
Wanted man in Kansas City, wanted man in Ohio,
Wanted man in Mississippi, wanted man in old Cheyenne,
Wherever you might look tonight, you might see this wanted man.

If Not for You

WORDS AND MUSIC BY
BOB DYLAN

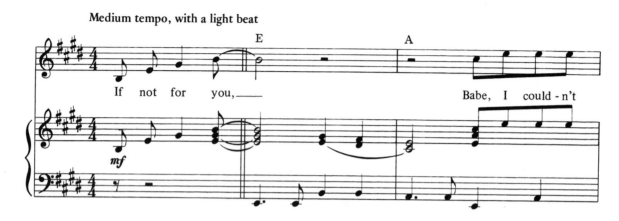

Medium tempo, with a light beat

If not for you, ____ Babe, I could - n't

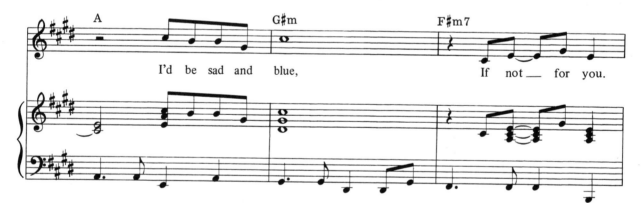

find the door, _ Could - n't e - ven see the floor, _

I'd be sad and blue, If not _ for you.

If not for you, _

Babe, I'd lay a - wake all night,_ Wait for the

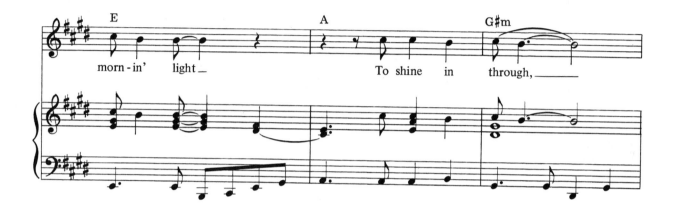

morn - in' light _ To shine in through,_____

But it would not be new,_____ If not for you.

A   E   B

If not for you   My sky would fall,   Rain would gath-er   too. __
If not for you   My sky would fall,   Rain would gath-er   too. __

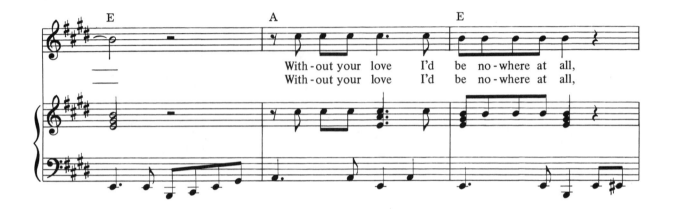

E   A   E

__ With-out your love   I'd   be no-where at all,
__ With-out your love   I'd   be no-where at all,

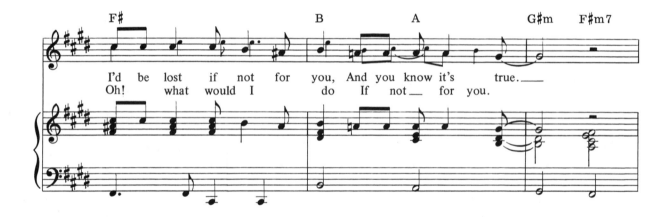

F#   B   A   G#m   F#m7

I'd be lost if not for you, And you know it's   true. __
Oh!   what would I   do If not __ for you.

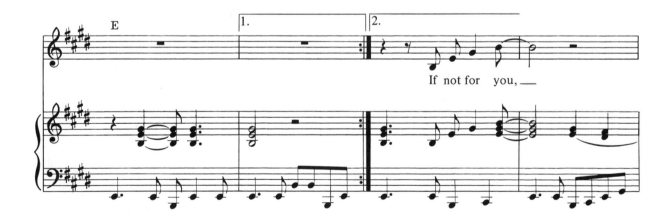

E   1.   2.

If not for you, __

All the Tired Horses

WORDS AND MUSIC BY
BOB DYLAN

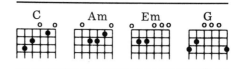

Woogie-Boogie

MUSIC BY
BOB DYLAN

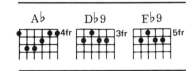

Medium Boogie

Minstrel Boy

WORDS AND MUSIC BY
BOB DYLAN

And now he's stuck on _____ top of _____ the hill. _____
Might - y Mock-ing - bird, _____ he still has such a heav - y load. _____

With twelve for - ward gears, it's been a long hard climb, And with
Be - neath his bound - 'ries, _____ what more can I tell, With

all of them la - dies, though, he's lone - ly still. _____
all of his trav - 'lin', but I'm still

on that road. _____

save his soul?

Living the Blues

WORDS AND MUSIC BY

BOB DYLAN

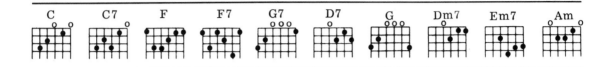

Moderate Shuffle

Since you've been gone___ I've been walk - ing a - round___ With my
have to go far ____ To know where you are,____

head bowed   down_ to my shoes.. I've been liv - ing the blues _____
Stran - gers all give_ me the news. I've been liv - ing the blues _____

1. Ev - 'ry night __ with-out you. _____ I don't

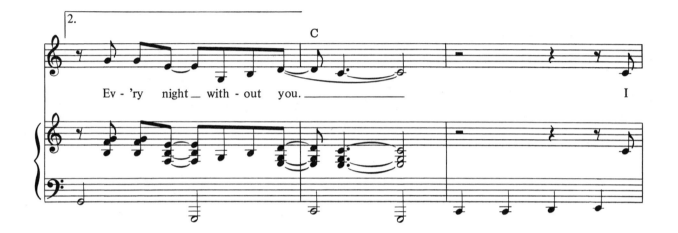

2. Ev - 'ry night __ with - out you. _____ I

think that it's best, __ I soon get some rest __ And for-get my pride.__

_____ But I can't de - ny__ This feel - ing that I __

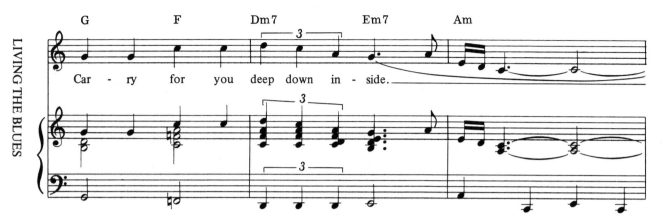

Car - ry for you deep down in - side.___

___ If you see me this way,___ You'd come back and you'd stay,___ Oh, how___

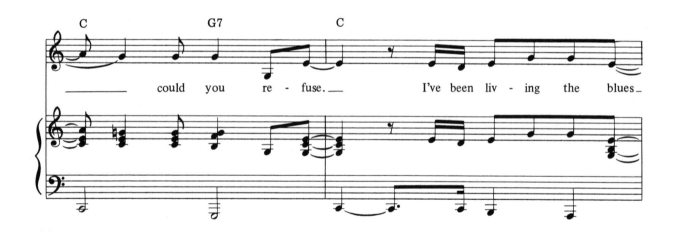

___ could you re - fuse.___ I've been liv - ing the blues___

___ Ev - 'ry night___ with - out you.___

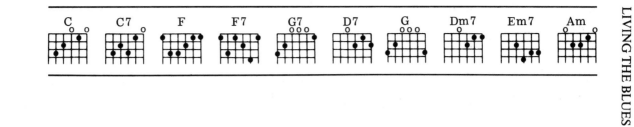

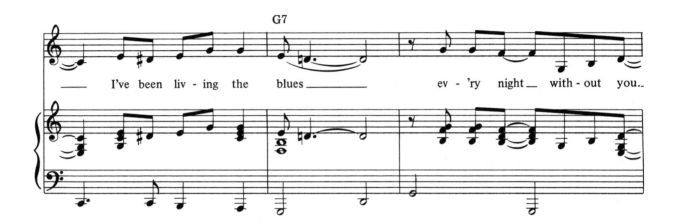

I've been liv - ing the blues _____ ev - 'ry night __ with - out you.__

I've been liv - ing the blues _____

ev - 'ry night __ with - out you. _____

Wigwam

MUSIC BY
BOB DYLAN

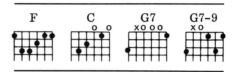

Moderately slow

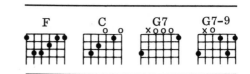

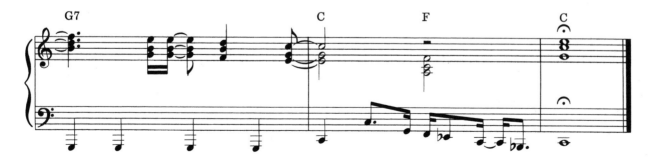

The Man in Me

WORDS AND MUSIC BY
BOB DYLAN

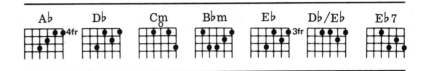

Moderately slow, with a beat

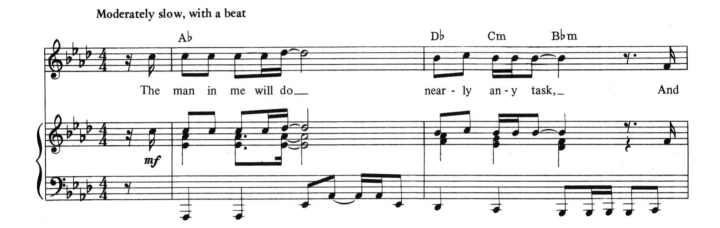

The man in me will do__ near-ly an-y task,__ And

as for com-pen-sa-tion, there's__ lit-tle he__ would ask.__ Take a

wom-an like you__ To get through__ to the man in me._____

THE MAN IN ME

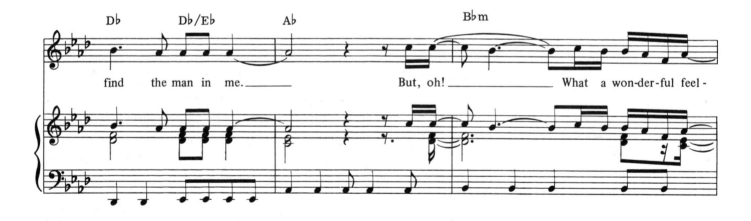

One More Weekend

WORDS AND MUSIC BY
BOB DYLAN

Moderately slow Blues, with a feeling of 12/8

Slip-pin' and __ slid-in' like a wea-sel on the run,
Com-in' and __ go-in' like a rab-bit in the wood,

I'm look-in' good to see you, yeah, __ and we can have some fun. __
I'm hap-py just to see you, yeah, __ look-in' so good.

One more week-end, __ one more week-end __ with you, __
One more week-end, __ one more week-end __ with you, __

one more week - end___ with you.___
one more week - end___ with you,___

One more week - end, one more week - end 'll do.___

We'll fly the night a - way, Hang out the whole next day,___

Things will be o - kay,___ You wait and see.___

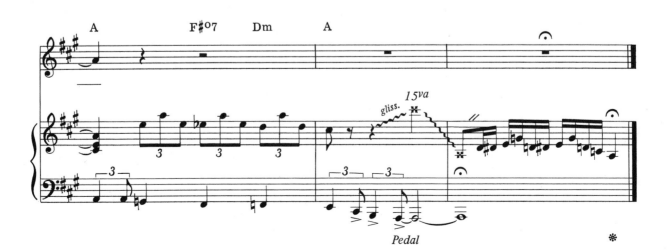

Time Passes Slowly

WORDS AND MUSIC BY
BOB DYLAN

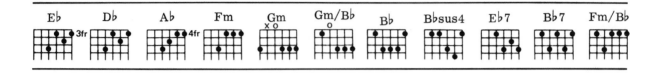

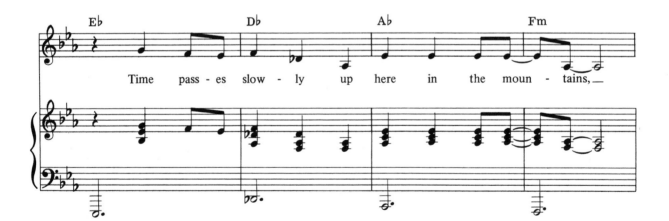

Time pass - es slow - ly up here in the moun - tains, ___

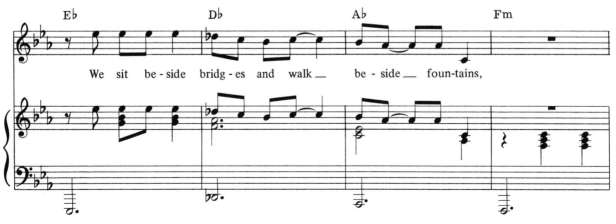

We sit be - side bridg - es and walk ___ be - side ___ foun-tains,

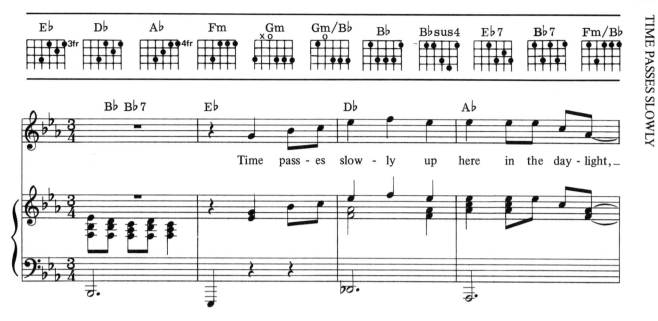

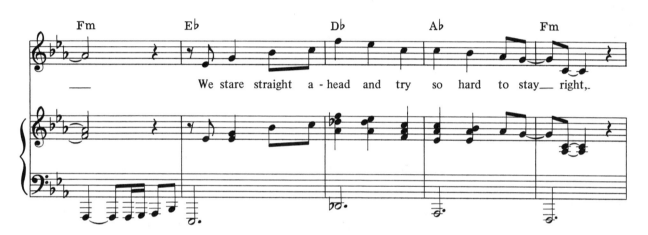

Time pass - es slow - ly up here in the day - light,__

We stare straight a - head and try so hard to stay__ right,_

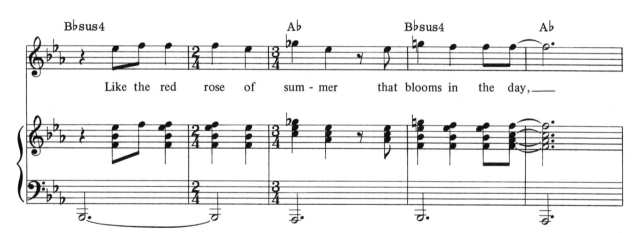

Like the red rose of sum - mer that blooms in the day,__

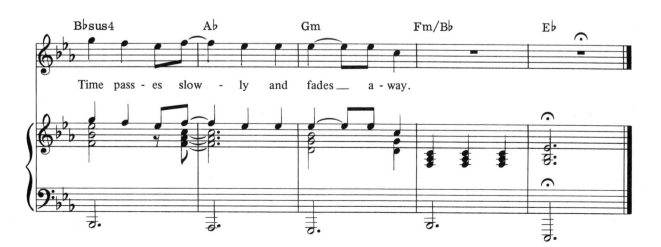

Time pass - es slow - ly and fades__ a - way.

Went to See the Gypsy

WORDS AND MUSIC BY
BOB DYLAN

Went to see the gyp-sy, Stay-in' in a big ho-tel.

He smiled when he saw me com-ing, And he said,

"Well,— well,— well." His room was dark ___ and crowd-

ed, Lights were low_ and dim.

"How are you?"_____ he said ___ to me,_____ I

said it back to him.___

I went down to the lob-by

To make a small_ call_ out.

A pret - ty danc - ing girl_

_ was there,_ And she _ be-gan to shout,

"Go on_ back_

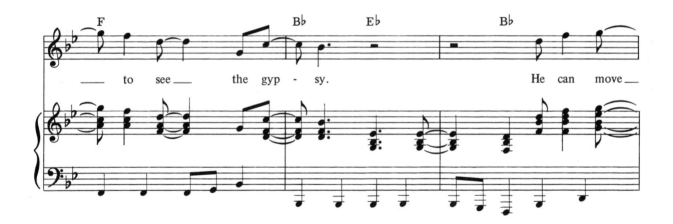

_ to see _ the gyp - sy.

He can move_

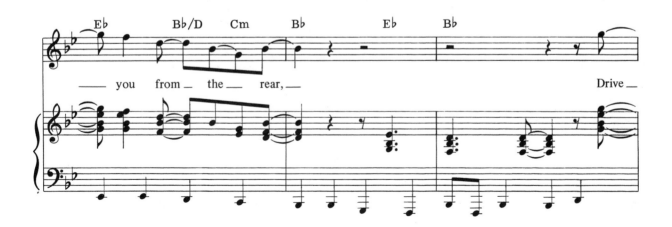

_ you from_ the_ rear,_

Drive_

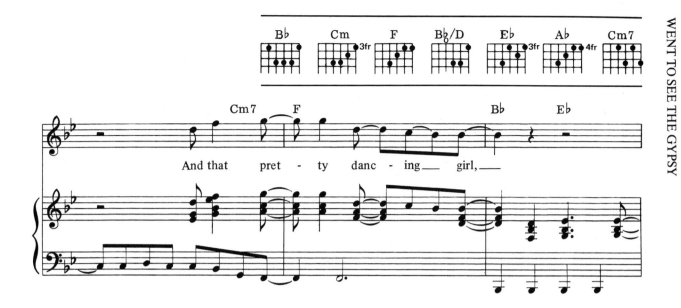

And that pret - ty danc - ing___ girl,___

She could not___ be found.___ So I

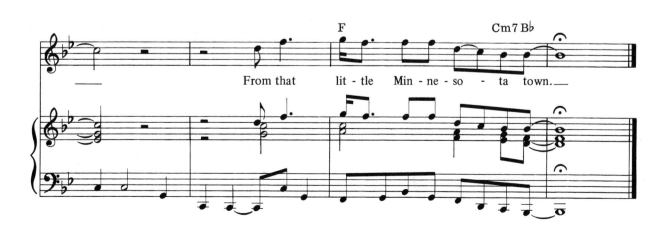

watched that sun___ come ris - ing From that lit - tle Min - ne - so - ta town.___

From that lit - tle Min - ne - so - ta town.___

Winterlude

WORDS AND MUSIC BY
BOB DYLAN

Moderately bright Waltz

Win - ter - lude, Win - ter - lude, _____ oh _____ dar - lin',
lude, Win - ter - lude, _____ my lit - tle ap - ple,
lude, Win - ter - lude, _____ my lit - tle dai - sy,

Win - ter - lude by the road to - night. _____
Win - ter - lude by the corn in the field,
Win - ter - lude by the tel - e - phone wire,

To - night there will be no quar - rel - in',
Win - ter - lude, let's go down to the chap - el,
Win - ter - lude, it's down mak - in' me la - zy, _____

Ev - 'ry - thing _____ is gon - na be al - right. _____
Then come back and cook up _____ a meal. _____
Come on, sit by the logs in _____ the fire. _____

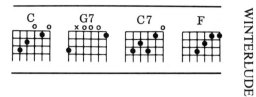

Oh, I see by the an - gel be - side me
Well, come out when the skat - ing rink glis - tens
The moon - light re - flects from the win - dow

That love has _____ a rea - son _____ to shine. _____
By the sun, near _____ the old cross - roads sign. _____
Where the snow - flakes, _____ they cov - er _____ the sand. _____

You're the one I _____ a - dore, come o - ver here and give me more, Then Win - ter -
The snow is _____ so cold, but our love can be bold, Win - ter -
Come out _____ to - night, ev - 'ry thing will be tight, Win - ter -

lude, this dude thinks you're fine. _____ Win - ter -
lude, don't be rude, please be mine. _____ Win - ter -
lude, this dude thinks you're grand. _____

If Dogs Run Free

WORDS AND MUSIC BY

BOB DYLAN

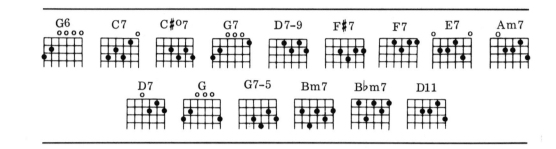

Moderate Blues

G6
(Spoken:) If dogs run free,   then why   not   we   Across the swooping plain?
If dogs run free,   why   not   me   Across the swamp of time?
If dogs run free,   then what must be,   Must be, and that is

C7   C#°7   D7-9
My ears hear   a symphony
My mind weaves   a   symphony   And
all.   True love can make a blade of grass

G7   F#7   F7   E7   Am7
Of two mules, trains and   rain.   The best is always
tapestry   of rhyme.   Oh, winds which rush my tale to
Stand up straight   and   tall.   In harmony

D7   G   Am7   D7–9

yet to come,   That's what they explain to me.
thee   So it may flow and   be,
with the cosmic sea,   True love needs no company,

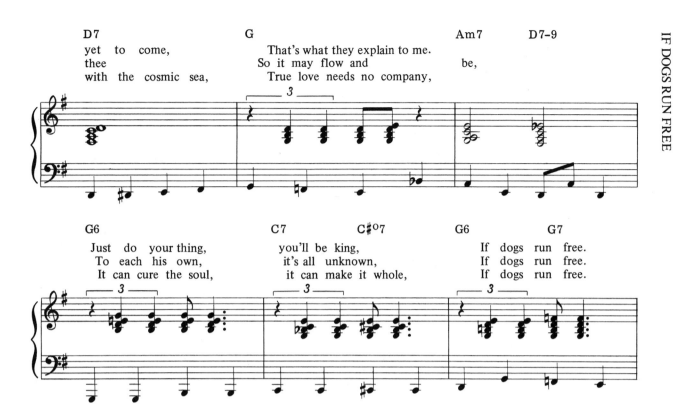

G6   C7   C♯°7   G6   G7

Just do your thing,   you'll be king,   If dogs run free.
To each his own,   it's all unknown,   If dogs run free.
It can cure the soul,   it can make it whole,   If dogs run free.

                   G7–5   C7   C♯°7

G   Bm7   B♭m7   Am7

D7   G   E7   1. Am7   D11   2. *D. C. and fade on instrumental*   Am7   D11

New Morning

WORDS AND MUSIC BY
BOB DYLAN

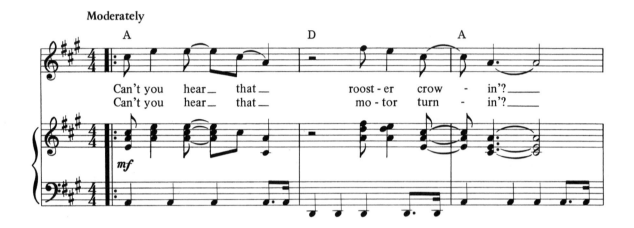

Moderately

Can't you hear that roost-er crow-in'?
Can't you hear that mo-tor turn-in'?

Rab-bit run-nin' down a-cross the road
Au-to-mo-bile com-in' in-to style

Un-der-neath the bridge where the wa-ter flowed through.
Com-in' down the road for a coun-try mile or

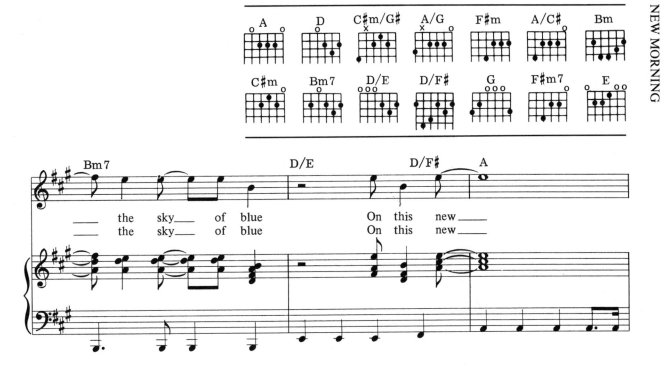

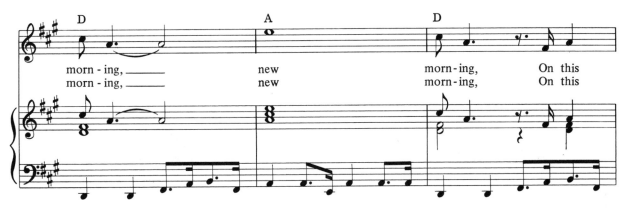

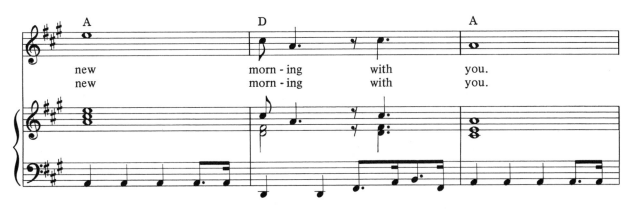

Three Angels

WORDS AND MUSIC BY
BOB DYLAN

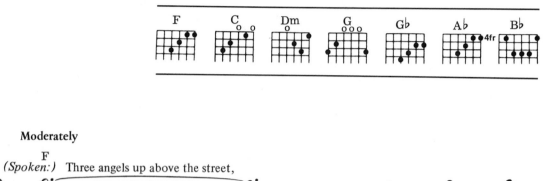

Moderately

(Spoken:) Three angels up above the street,

mp

With Pedal Throughout

Each one playing a horn,

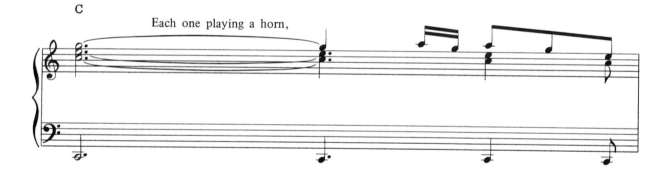

Dressed in green robes with wings that stick out,

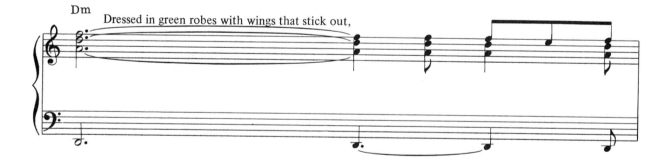

They've been there since Christmas morn.

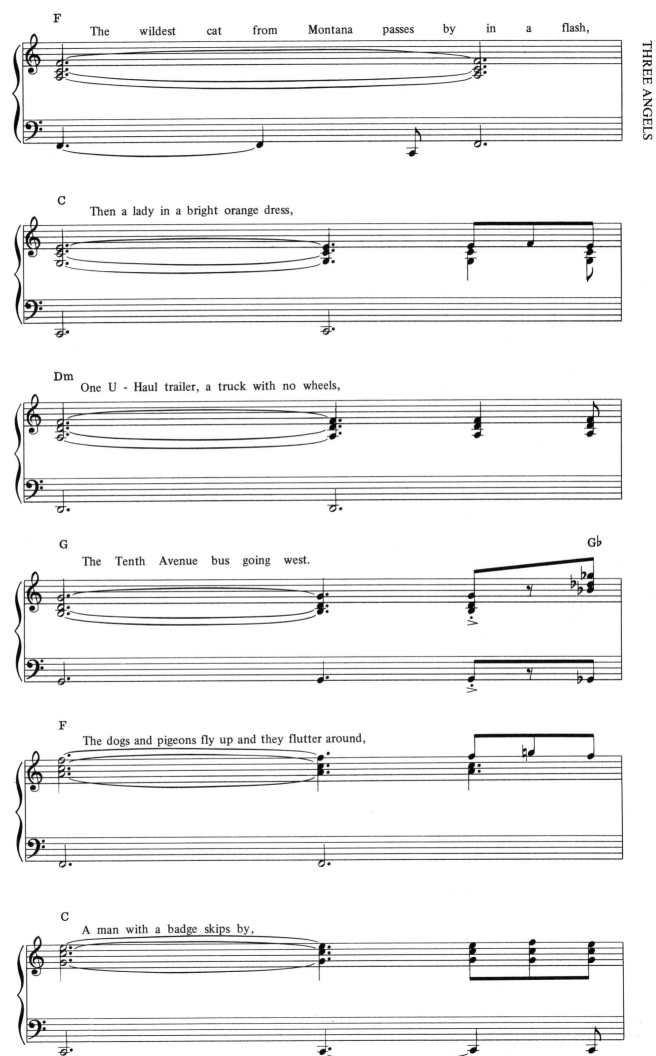

Dm

Three fellas crawlin' on their way back to work,

G

Nobody stops to ask why.   **G♭**

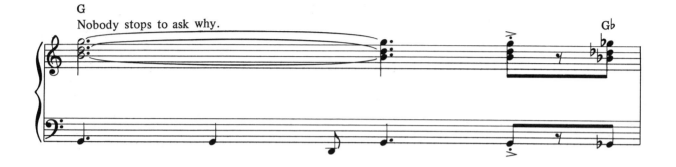

F

The bakery truck stops outside of that fence

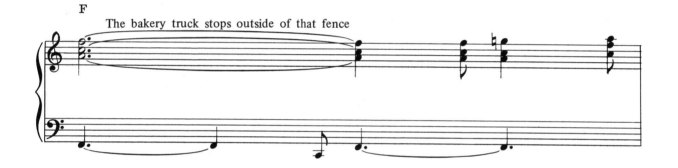

C

Where the angels stand high on their poles,

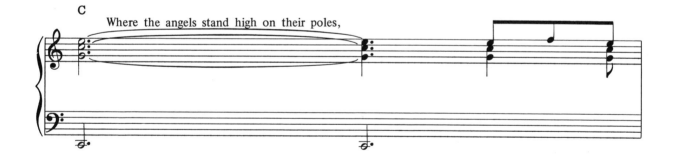

Dm

The driver peeks out, trying to find one face

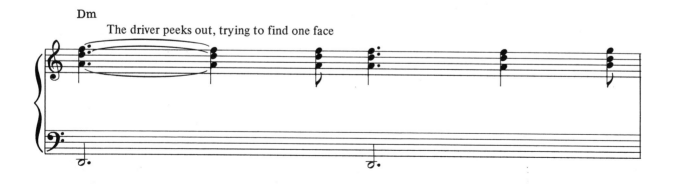

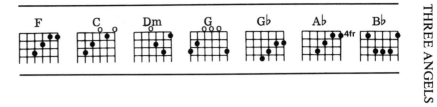

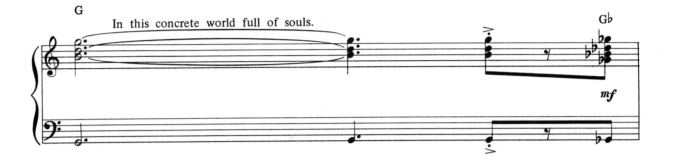

In this concrete world full of souls.

The angels play on their horns all day,

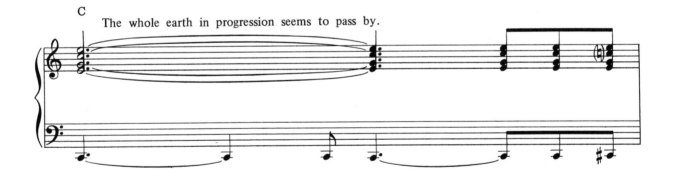

The whole earth in progression seems to pass by.

But does anyone hear the music they play, Does anyone even try?

Father of Night

WORDS AND MUSIC BY
BOB DYLAN

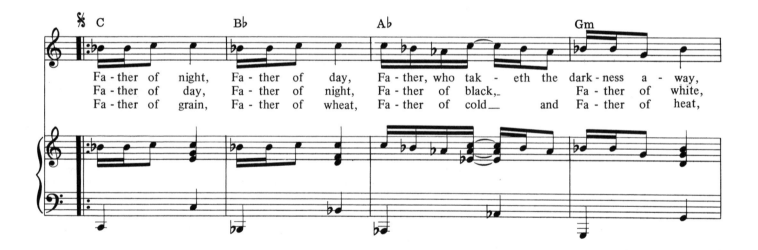

Father of night, Father of day, Father, who tak-eth the dark-ness a-way,
Father of day, Father of night, Father of black,_ Father of white,
Father of grain, Father of wheat, Father of cold_ and Father of heat,

Fa-ther, who teach-eth the bird to fly, _ Build-er of rain-bows_
Fa-ther, who build the moun-tain so high,_ Who shap-eth the cloud_
Fa-ther of air and Fa-ther of trees,_ Who

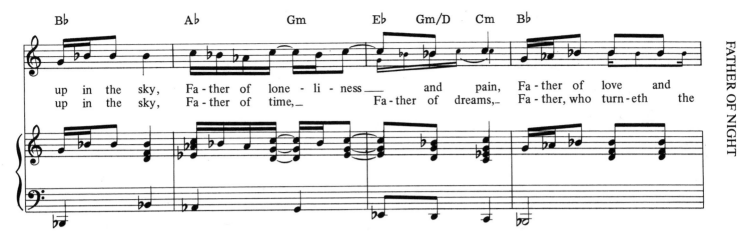

up in the sky, Fa-ther of lone-li-ness___ and pain, Fa-ther of love and
up in the sky, Fa-ther of time,___ Fa-ther of dreams,___ Fa-ther, who turn-eth the

1. Fa-ther of rain.
2. *D. S. al Coda* 𝄋 riv-ers and streams.

Coda ⊕ dwells in our hearts and our mem-o-ries,___

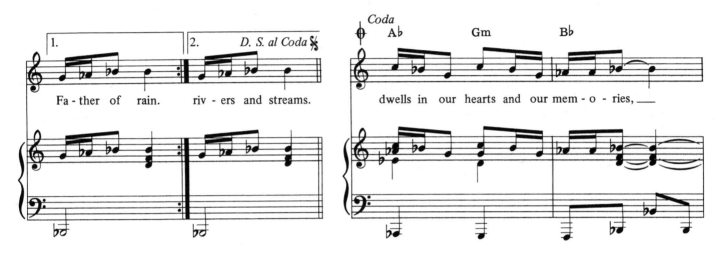

Fa-ther of min-utes, Fa-ther of days, Fa-ther of whom we most

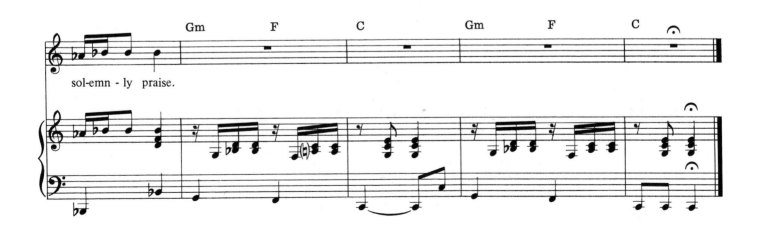

sol-emn-ly praise.

I'd Have You Any Time

WORDS AND MUSIC BY
BOB DYLAN AND GEORGE HARRISON

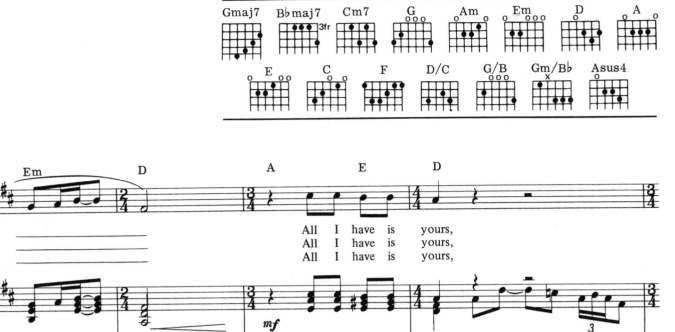

All I have is yours,
All I have is yours,
All I have is yours,

All you see is mine ⎯⎯⎯ And I'm glad to have you in my arms,
All you see is mine ⎯⎯⎯ And I'm glad to have you in my arms,
All you see is mine ⎯⎯⎯ And I'm glad to have you in my arms,

1.2.

I'd have you an - y time.
I'd have you an - y time.

3.

I'd have you an - y time.

When I Paint My Masterpiece

WORDS AND MUSIC BY
BOB DYLAN

Oh, the streets of Rome are filled with rub-ble,_ An-cient foot-
hours I've spent_ in-side the Col - i - se - um,_ Dodg-ing li-
Rome and land-ed in Brus-sels,_ On a plane_

prints ____ are ev-'ry-where._ You can
ons ____ and wast-in' time._ Oh, those
___ ride so bump-y that I al-most cried.

al-most think ____ that you're see - in' dou-ble ____ On a
might-y kings of the jun-gle, I could hard-ly stand to see 'em,_ Yes, it
Cler-gy-men in un - i-form and young girls pull-in' mus-cles,_ Ev-'ry-

cold, dark night_ on the Span-ish Stairs. ____
sure has been_ a long, hard climb. ____
one was there to greet me when I stepped in - side. ____

WHEN I PAINT MY MASTERPIECE

Sign on the Window

WORDS AND MUSIC BY
BOB DYLAN

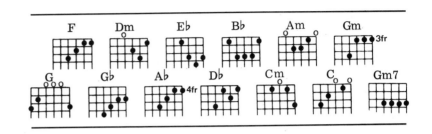

Sign on the win - dow says __ "Lone - ly,"

Sign on the door said "No Com - pa - ny __ Al - lowed," __

Sign on the street says "Y' Don't Own __ Me,"

Sign on the porch says "Three's A Crowd,"— Sign on the porch says

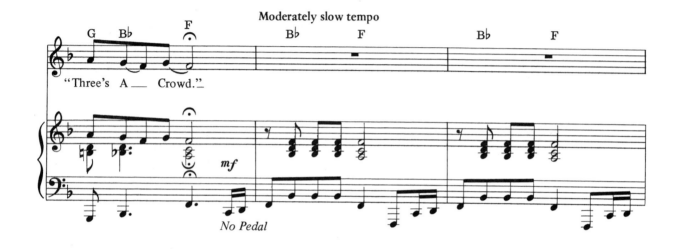

Moderately slow tempo

"Three's A — Crowd."

No Pedal

Freely

Her and her boy-friend went to Cal-i-

rit. *With Pedal*

for - ia, Her and her boy - friend

Looks like a-noth-ing but ____ rain. . . ____

Sure gon-na be wet to-night ___ on ___ Main Street. . .

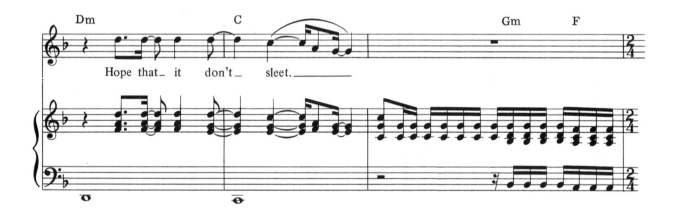

Hope that ___ it don't ___ sleet. _____

Day of the Locusts

WORDS AND MUSIC BY

BOB DYLAN

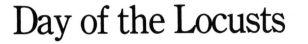

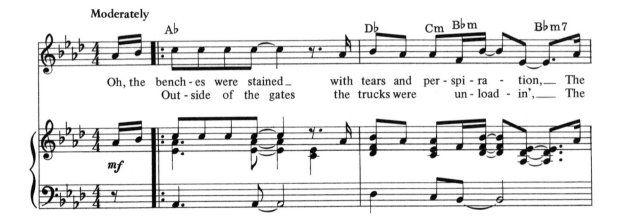

Oh, the bench - es were stained with tears and per - spi - ra - tion, The
Out - side of the gates the trucks were un - load - in', The

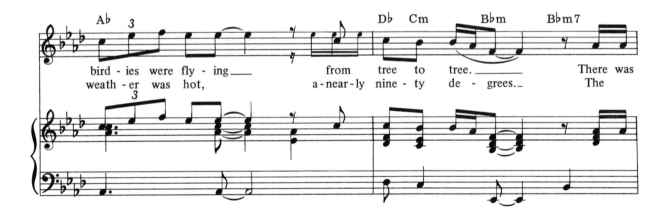

bird - ies were fly - ing from tree to tree. There was
weath - er was hot, a - near - ly nine - ty de - grees. The

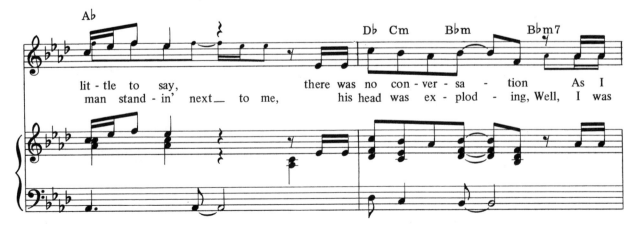

lit - tle to say, there was no con - ver - sa - tion As I
man stand - in' next to me, his head was ex - plod - ing, Well, I was

stepped to the stage___ to pick up my de-gree.___ And the
pray - in' the piec - es would-n't fall on me. ___ Yeah, the

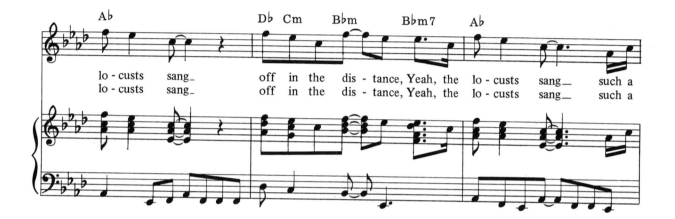

lo - custs sang_ off in the dis - tance, Yeah, the lo - custs sang__ such a
lo - custs sang_ off in the dis - tance, Yeah, the lo - custs sang__ such a

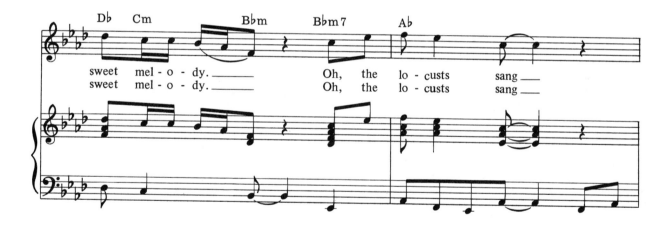

sweet mel - o - dy._____ Oh, the lo - custs sang__
sweet mel - o - dy._____ Oh, the lo - custs sang__

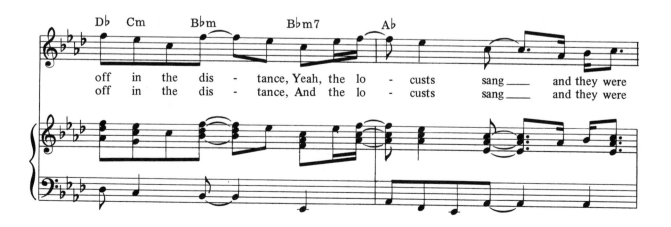

off in the dis - tance, Yeah, the lo - custs sang____ and they were
off in the dis - tance, And the lo - custs sang____ and they were

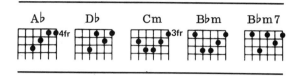

al - read - y walk - in', But the next time I looked__ there was
hills of Da - ko - ta, Sure was glad__ to get

light in the room.__ And the lo - custs sang, yeah, it
out of there a - live. And the lo - custs sang, well, it

give me a chill, Oh,__ the lo - custs sang__ such a
give me a chill, Yeah,__ the lo - custs sang__ such a

Watching the River Flow

WORDS AND MUSIC BY
BOB DYLAN

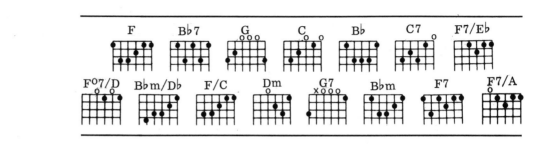

Moderate Blues

What's the mat - ter with me,_____ I don't have
Wish I was back in the cit - y_____ In - stead of this

much to say,_____ With the
old bank of sand,_____ sun

Day-light sneak-in' through the win - dow And I'm still in this all-
beat-ing down o - ver the chim-ney tops_____ And the one I love_____ so close at

riv - er flow, ____ Watch - in' the

riv - er flow, ____ Watch - in' the

riv - er flow, ____ But I'll sit down on ____ this bank of ____

sand And watch the riv - er flow. ____

molto rit.

Knockin' on Heaven's Door

WORDS AND MUSIC BY
BOB DYLAN

Ma - ma, take this badge off of me
Ma - ma, put my guns in the ground

I can't use__ it an - y more__
I can't shoot__ them__ an - y more__

It's get - tin' dark,__ too dark__ for me to see
That long black__ cloud is__ com - in' down__

I feel like I'm knock-in' on heav-en's door.__
I feel like I'm knock-in' on heav-en's door.__

No Pedal

George Jackson

WORDS AND MUSIC BY

BOB DYLAN

Moderately fast

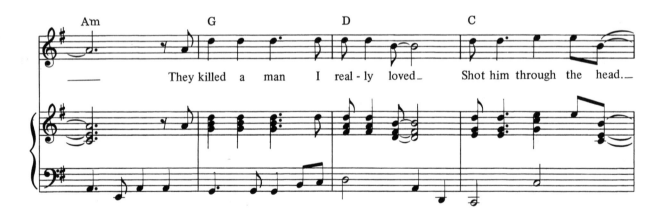

1. I woke up this morn - in' There were tears ___ in my bed, ___

They killed a man I real - ly loved ___ Shot him through the head. ___

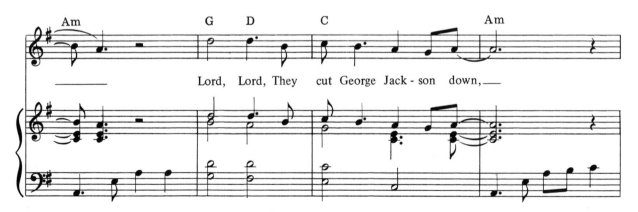

Lord, Lord, They cut George Jack - son down, ___

G   D   C   G

Lord, Lord, They laid him in —— the ground.

2.
G | D
Sent him off to prison
  | C | Am |
For a seventy dollar robbery
G | D
Closed the door behind him
  | C | Am |
And they threw away the key
G   D
Lord, Lord
  | C | Am |
They cut George Jackson down
G   D
Lord, Lord
  | C | G | ||
They laid him in the ground

3.
G | D
He wouldn't take shit from no one
  | C | Am |
He wouldn't bow down or kneel
  | G | D
Authorities, they hated him
  | C | Am |
Because he was just too real
G   D
Lord, Lord
  | C | Am |
They cut George Jackson down
G   D
Lord, Lord,
  | C | G | ||
They laid him in the ground

4.
G | D
Prison guards they cursed him
  | C | Am
As they watched him from above
     | G | D
But they were frightened of his power
    | C | Am |
They were scared of his love
G   D
Lord, Lord
  | C | Am |
So they cut George Jackson down
G   D
Lord, Lord
   | C | G | ||
They laid him in the ground

5.
G | D
Sometimes I think this whole world
  | C | Am |
Is one big prison-yard
G | D
Some of us are prisoners
   | C | Am |
The rest of us are guards
G   D
Lord, Lord
  | C | Am |
They cut George Jackson down
G   D
Lord, Lord
  | C | G | ||
They laid him in the ground

Wallflower

WORDS AND MUSIC BY
BOB DYLAN

Wall-flow'r, wall-flow'r, Won't you dance with me? I'm sad and lone-ly, too. Wall-flow'r, wall-flow'r, Won't you dance with me? I'm fall-in' in love with you.

Just like you I'm won-d'rin' what I'm do-in' here.
I have seen you stand-ing in the smok-ey haze

Billy

WORDS AND MUSIC BY
BOB DYLAN

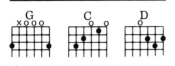

Moderately

1. There's guns a-cross the riv - er aim - in' at ya

Law - man on your trail, ___ he'd like to catch ___ ya ___

Boun - ty hunt - ers, too, ___ they'd like to get ___

___ ya ___   Bil - ly, they don't like ___

_____ you to be _____ so free. _____

2. **G**
Campin' out all night on the berenda
Dealin' cards 'til dawn in the hacienda
C **|G**
Up to Boot Hill they'd like to send ya
D **|G**
Billy don't you turn your back on me

3. **G**
Playin' around with some sweet señorita
Into her dark hallway she will lead ya
C **|G**
In some lonesome shadows she will greet ya
D **|G**
Billy you're so far away from home

4. **G**
There's eyes behind the mirrors in empty places
Bullet holes and scars between the spaces
|C **|G**
There's always one more notch and ten more paces
D **|G**
Billy and you're walkin' all alone

5. **G**
They say that Pat Garrett's got your number
So sleep with one eye open when you slumber
C **|G**
Every little sound just might be thunder
D **|G**
Thunder from the barrel of his gun

6. **G**
Guitars will play your grand finale
Down in some Tularosa alley
C **|G**
Maybe in the Rio Pecos valley
D **|G**
Billy you're so far away from home

7. **G**
There's always some new stranger sneakin' glances
Some trigger-happy fool willin' to take chances
C **|G**
And some old whore from San Pedro to make advances
|D **|G**
Advances on your spirit and your soul

8. **G**
The businessmen from Taos want you to go down
They've hired Pat Garrett to force a showdown
C **|G**
Billy don't it make ya feel so lowdown
|D **|G**
To be shot down by the man who was your friend

9. **G**
Hang on to your woman if you got one
Remember in El Paso, once, you shot one
|C **|G**
She may have been a whore, but she was a hot one
D **|G**
Billy you been runnin' for so long

10. **G**
Guitars will play your grand finale
Down in some Tularosa alley
C **|G**
Maybe in the Rio Pecos valley
D **|G**
Billy you're so far away from home

Forever Young

WORDS AND MUSIC BY
BOB DYLAN

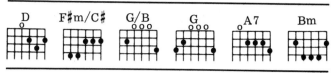

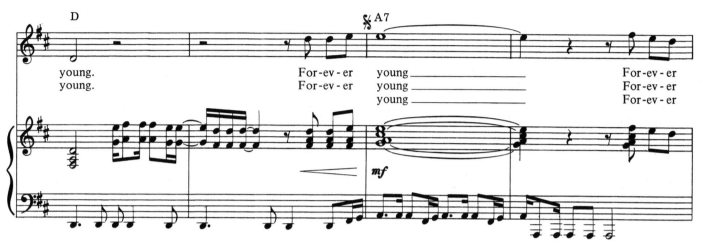

have a strong foun - da-tion When the winds of chang - es shift.

May your heart al - ways be joy - ful May your

song al - ways_ be sung May you stay for - ev - er young.___

D. S. al Coda 𝄋

For-ev - er

𝄌 *Coda*

young.___

rit.

On a Night Like This

WORDS AND MUSIC BY
BOB DYLAN

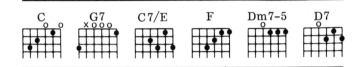

Medium beat

On a night like this _____
So glad you've come to stay_
I can't get an - y sleep_

So glad you came a - round_

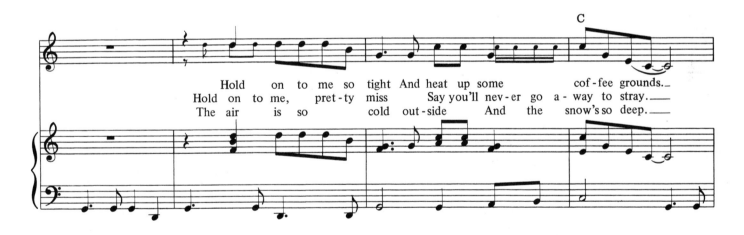

Hold on to me so tight And heat up some cof - fee grounds._
Hold on to me, pret - ty miss Say you'll nev - er go a - way to stray._
The air is so cold out - side And the snow's so deep._

We got much to talk a - bout_ And much to rem - i - nisce_
Run your fin - gers down my spine_ Bring me a touch of bliss_
Build a fire, throw on logs_ And lis - ten to it hiss_

ON A NIGHT LIKE THIS

Let the four winds blow _____ A - round this old ___ cab - in door___

If I'm not too___ far off ___ I think we did this once be - fore.

There's more frost on ___ the win-dow glass___ With each new ten-der kiss ___

___ But it sure feels right ___ On a night___ like this.___

Going, Going, Gone

WORDS AND MUSIC BY
BOB DYLAN

I've just reached a place Where the wil-low don't bend

There's not much more to be said It's the top of the end I'm go-ing

I'm go-ing I'm gone.

I'm clos-in' the book On the pag-es and the text And I don't real-ly care What

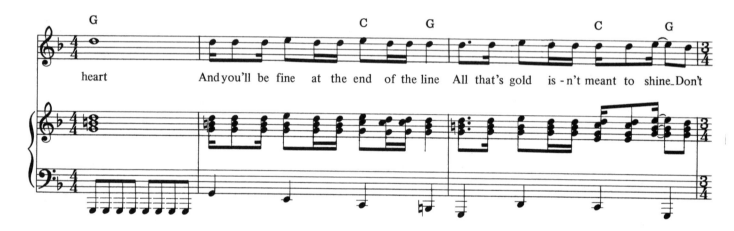

gone___

Grand-ma said, "Boy, go and fol-low your

heart___ And you'll be fine at the end of the line All that's gold is-n't meant to shine. Don't

D. S. al Coda

you and your one___ true love___ ev - er part."___

go - ing___ I'm gone.___

Tough Mama

WORDS AND MUSIC BY
BOB DYLAN

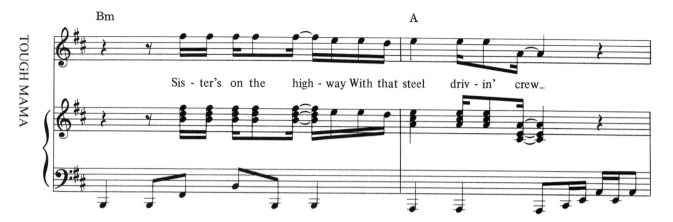

Sis - ter's on the high - way With that steel driv - in' crew__

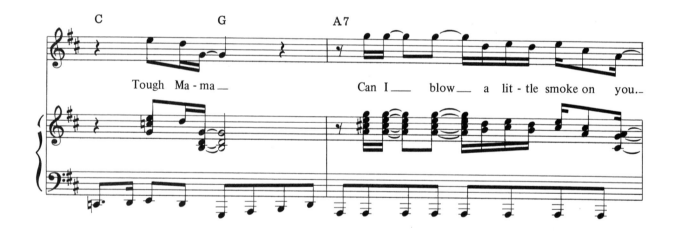

Pa - pa's in the big__ house His work - in' days__ are through.__

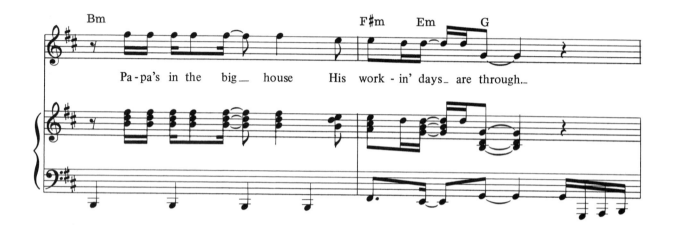

Tough Ma - ma__ Can I__ blow__ a lit - tle smoke on you.__

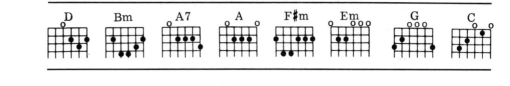

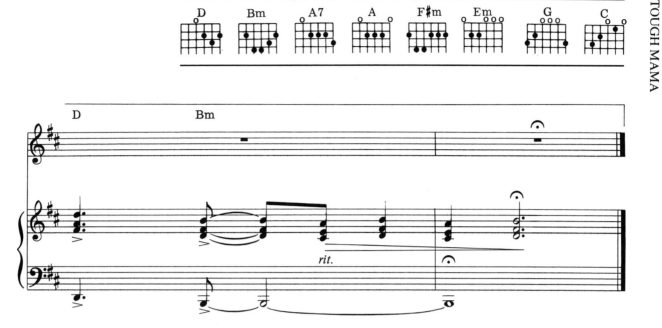

2. Dark Beauty

D   Bm |

A7 | |
Won't you move it on over and make some room
D   Bm |
It's my duty
A7 | |
To bring you down to the field where the flowers bloom
Bm |
Ashes in the furnace
A |
Dust on the rise
Bm |
You came through it all the way
F#m   Em   G |
Flyin' through the skies
C   G
Dark Beauty
   |A7 | ||
With that long night's journey in your eyes

3. Sweet Goddess

D   Bm |

A7 | |
Born of a blinding light and a changing wind
D   Bm |
Now, don't be modest
A7 | |
You know who you are and where you've been
Bm |
Jack, the Cowboy, went up north
A |
He's buried in your past
Bm
The Lone Wolf went out drinking
   |F#m Em   G |
That was over pretty fast
C   G
Sweet Goddess
   |A7 | ||
Your perfect stranger's comin' in at last

4. Silver Angel

D   Bm |

A7 | |
With the badge of the lonesome road sewed into your sleeve
D   Bm
I'd be grateful
   |A7 | |
If this golden ring you would receive
Bm
Today on the countryside
     |A
It was a-hotter than a crotch
|Bm
I stood alone upon the ridge
   |F#mEm   G |
And all I did was watch
C   G
Sweet Goddess
   |A7 | ||
It must be time to carve another notch

5. I'm crestfallen

     |A7 | |
The world of illusion is at my door
D   Bm |
I ain't a-haulin'
A7 |
Any of my lambs to the market place anymore
   |Bm
The prison walls are crumblin'
   |A |
There is no end in sight
Bm
I've gained some recognition
   |F#m   Em G |
But I lost my appetite
C   G |
Dark Beauty
A7 | |D   Bm | ||
Meet me at the border late tonight

Hazel

WORDS AND MUSIC BY
BOB DYLAN

Moderately, with a two feel

Ha - zel, dirt - y blonde hair,

I would-n't be a-shamed to be seen with you an - y-where.

You got some-thing I want____ plen - ty of____

Ooh,____ a lit - tle touch of your love.____

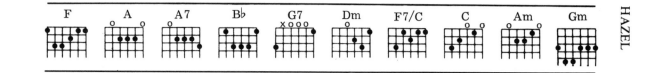

HAZEL

Oh, no, I don't___ need an-y re-mind - er___

To know__ how much I real - ly care.___

But it's just mak - ing me blind - er and blind - er___ Be-cause I'm

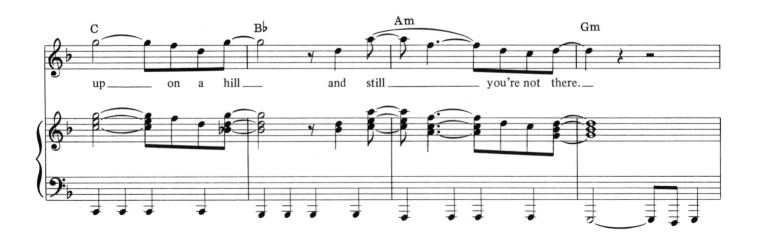

up___ on a hill___ and still___ you're not there.__

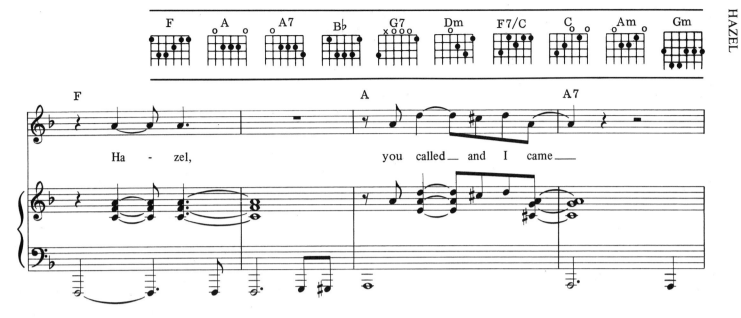

Ha - zel, you called and I came

Now don't make me play this wait - ing game.

You've got some-thing I want plen - ty of

Ooh, a lit - tle touch of your love.

Something There Is About You

WORDS AND MUSIC BY
BOB DYLAN

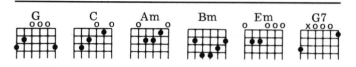

Some-thing there is a-bout_ you / That strikes a match in me._
Thought I'd shak - en the won - der / And the phan - toms of _ my youth._
Some-thing there is a-bout_ you / That moves with style_ and grace._

Is it the way your bod - y moves
Rain - y days on the Great Lakes
I was in a whirl - wind

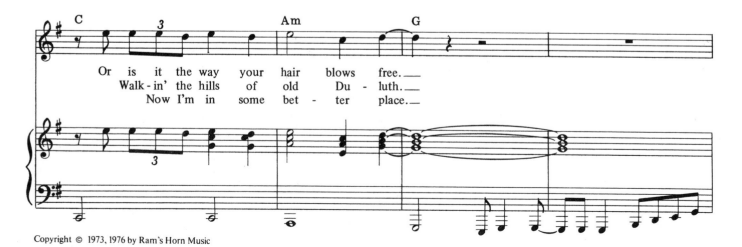

Or is it the way your hair blows free._
Walk - in' the hills of old Du - luth._
Now I'm in some bet - ter place._

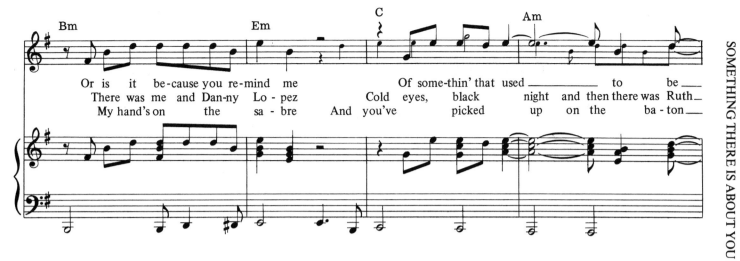

Or is it be-cause you re-mind me   Of some-thin' that used _____ to be
There was me and Dan-ny Lo - pez   Cold eyes, black   night and then there was Ruth
My hand's on   the   sa - bre   And you've   picked   up on the ba - ton

Some-thin' that's crossed   o - ver
Some-thin' there is a - bout _ you

From _____ an-oth-er cen - tu - ry. _____
That brings back a   long   for-got - ten   truth. _____

Sud-den-ly I found_

you And the spir - it in me sings.

Don't have to look no fur - ther You're the soul

of man - y things. I could say that I'd be

faith - ful I could say it in one sweet, eas - y breath.

Dirge

WORDS AND MUSIC BY
BOB DYLAN

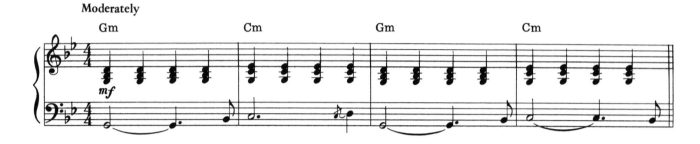

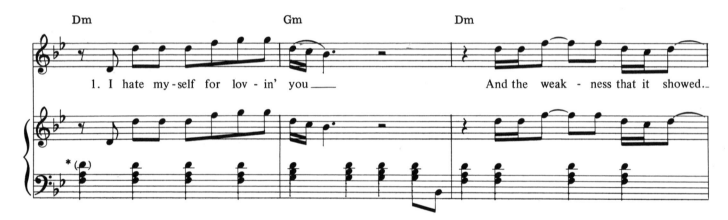

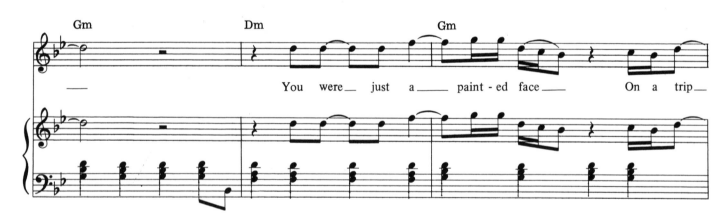

*( ) Indicates that the D note should be released quickly in order to play the D in the right hand.

lights went out   All a-round___ the old ho-tel_____

I hate my-self for lov-in' you___   And I'm glad___ the cur-tain fell._____

2.
| Dm | Gm | |
I hate that foolish game we played
| Dm | Gm | |
And the need that was expressed
| Dm | Gm | |
And the mercy that you showed to me
| Dm | Am | |
Whoever would have guessed
| Bb | Dm | |
I went out on Lower Broadway
| Gm | | |
And I felt that place within
| Bb | Eb |
That hollow place where martyrs weep
| Bb Cm | Gm ||
And angels play with sin

3.
| Dm | Gm | |
Heard your songs of freedom
| Dm | Gm | |
And man forever stripped
| Dm | Gm | |
Acting out his folly
| Dm | Am | |
While his back is being whipped
| Bb | Dm | |
Like a slave in orbit
| Gm | | |
He's beaten 'til he's tame
| Bb | Eb |
All for a moment's glory
| Bb Cm | Gm ||
And it's a dirty, rotten shame

4.
| Dm | Gm | |
There are those who worship loneliness
| Dm | Gm | |
I'm not one of them
| Dm | Gm | |
In this age of fiberglass
| Dm | Am | |
I'm searching for a gem
| Bb | Dm | |
The crystal ball up on the wall
| Gm | | |
Hasn't shown me nothing yet
| Bb | Eb |
I've paid the price of solitude
| Bb Cm | Gm ||
But at least I'm out of debt

5.
| Dm | Gm | |
Can't recall a useful thing
| Dm | Gm | |
You ever did for me
| Dm | Gm | |
'Cept pat me on the back one time
| Dm | Am | |
When I was on my knees
| Bb | Dm | |
We stared into each other's eyes
| Gm | | |
'Til one of us would break
| Bb | Eb |
No use to apologize
| Bb Cm | Gm ||
What diff'rence would it make

6.
| Dm | Gm | |
So sing your praise of progress
| Dm | Gm | |
And of the Doom Machine
| Dm | Gm | |
The naked truth is still tabu
| Dm | Am | |
Whenever it can be seen
| Bb | Dm | |
Lady Luck who shines on me
| Gm | | |
Will tell you where I'm at
| Bb | Eb |
I hate myself for lovin' you
| Bb Cm | Gm ||
But I should get over that

Never Say Goodbye

WORDS AND MUSIC BY
BOB DYLAN

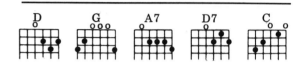

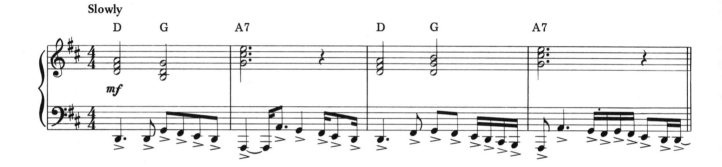

Twi - light on the fro - zen lake ____ North wind a - bout to

break On foot-prints in the snow Si - lence down be - low.

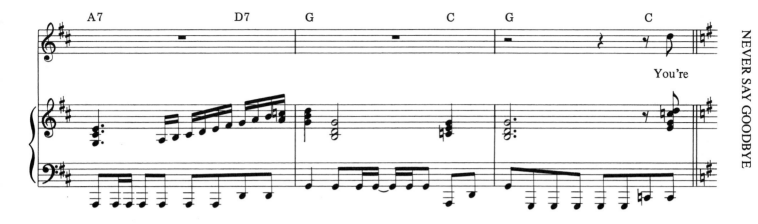

You're

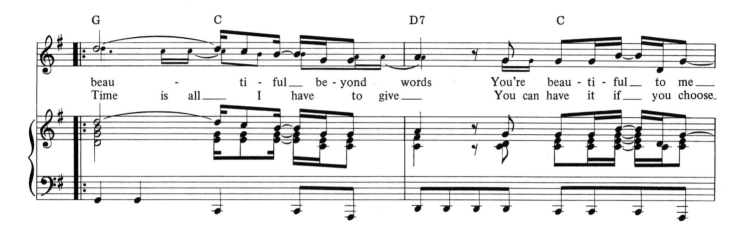

beau - ti - ful__ be - yond words   You're beau - ti - ful__ to me__
Time   is   all__ I   have   to give__   You can have it if__ you choose__

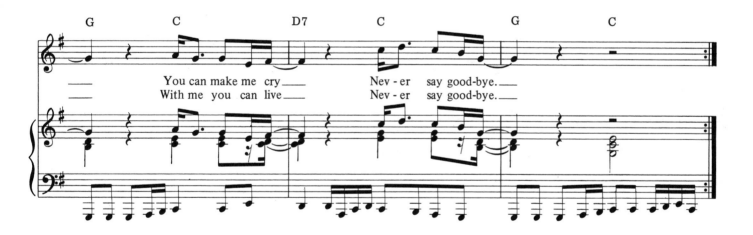

___ You can make me cry___   Nev - er   say good-bye.___
___ With me you can live___   Nev - er   say good-bye.___

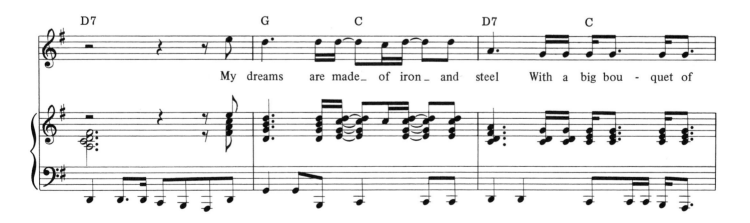

My dreams   are made_ of iron_ and steel   With a big bou - quet of

ros - es hang-ing down ___ From the heav-ens to the ground.___

The

crash - ing waves roll o - ver me ___ As I stand up-on the sand___

___ Wait for you to come ___ And grab hold of my hand.___

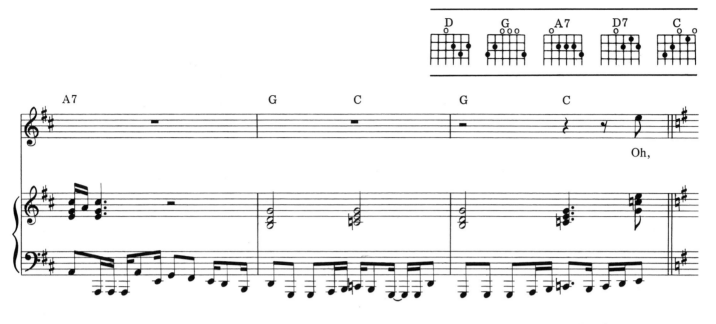

Oh,

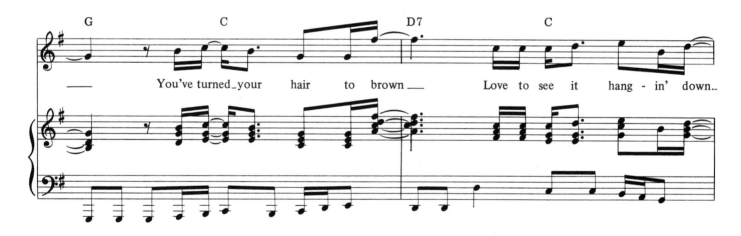

ba - by, ba - by, ba - by blue,___ You'll change your last ___ name too ___

You've turned your hair to brown ___ Love to see it hang - in' down ___

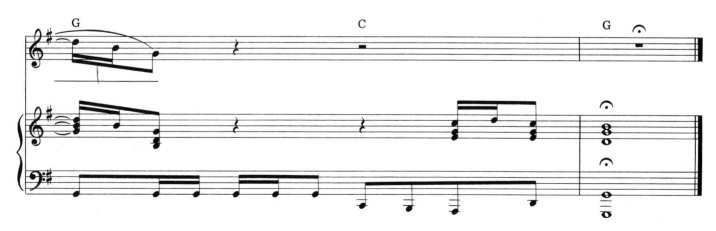

Wedding Song

WORDS AND MUSIC BY
BOB DYLAN

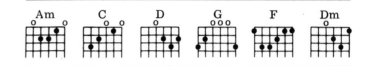

Moderately

1. I love you more_ than ev - er More than time and more than love_____ I

With Pedal Throughout

love you more than mon - ey And more than____ the stars a - bove.

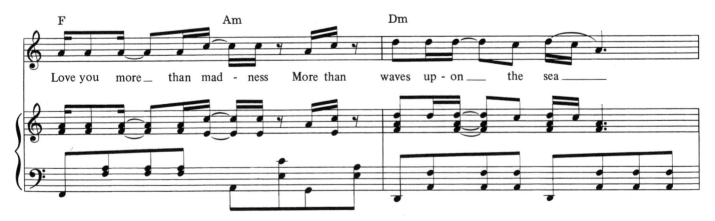

Love you more_ than mad - ness More than waves up - on____ the sea_____

Love you more_ than life it - self_ You mean_ that much_ to me._

2. Am   C
   Ever since you walked right in
     | D
   The circle's been complete
     | Am   C
   I've said goodbye to haunted rooms
     | G
   And faces in the street
     | F   C
   To the courtyard of the jester
     | Dm
   Which is hidden from the sun
   | Am   C
   I love you more than ever
     | G | ||
   And I haven't yet begun

3. Am   C
   You breathed on me and made my life
     | D
   A richer one to live
      | Am   C
   When I was deep in poverty
     | G |
   You taught me how to give
   F   C
   Dried the tears up from my dreams
     | Dm |
   And pulled me from the hole
   Am   C
   Quenched my thirst and satisfied
     | G | ||
   The burning in my soul

4. Am   C
   You gave me babies one, two, three
     | D |
   What is more, you saved my life
   Am   C
   Eye for eye and tooth for tooth
     | G
   Your love cuts like a knife
     | F   Am
   My thoughts of you don't ever rest
     | C   G
   They'd kill me if I lie
     | Am   C
   I'd sacrifice the world for you
     | G | ||
   And watch my senses die

5. Am   C
   The tune that is yours and mine
     | D
   To play upon this earth
     | Am   C |
   We'll play it out the best we know
   G
   Whatever it is worth
     | F   Am
   What's lost is lost, we can't regain
     | C   G   Dm
   What went down in the flood
     | Am   C
   But happiness to me is you
     | G | ||
   And I love you more than blood

6. It's never been my duty
     | D
   To remake the world at large
     | Am   C
   Nor is it my intention
     | G
   To sound a battle charge
         | F   Am
   'Cause I love you more than all of that
         | C   Dm
   With a love that doesn't bend
      | Am   C
   And if there is eternity
     | G | ||
   I'd love you there again

7. Am   C
   Oh, can't you see that you were born
     | Dm
   To stand by my side
     | Am   C
   And I was born to be with you
     | G
   You were born to be my bride
        | F   C |
   You're the other half of what I am
   Dm
   You're the missing piece
     | Am   C
   And I love you more than ever
     | G | ||
   With that love that doesn't cease

8. Am   C
   You turn the tide on me each day
     | Dm   D |
   And teach my eyes to see
   Am   C
   Just bein' next to you
     | G
   Is a natural thing for me
     | F   Am
   And I could never let you go
     | Dm
   No matter what goes on
     | Am   C
   'Cause I love you more than ever
     | G | ||
   Now that the past is gone

You Angel You

WORDS AND MUSIC BY
BOB DYLAN

Lyrics:

You an-gel you ___ You got me un-der your wing ___ The
You an-gel you ___ You're as fine as an-y-thing's fine ___ The

way you walk ___ and the way ___ you talk ___ I feel I could al-most sing. ___
way you walk ___ and the way ___ you talk ___ It

sure plays on my mind. ___ You know I ___ can't sleep ___ at night ___ for try-
know I ___ can't sleep ___ at night ___ for try-

ing
in'
Nev-er did feel_ this way_ be - fore_
Nev-er did feel_ this way_ be - fore_

To Coda

I get up at night and walk_ the floor_ If this is love then gim-me more And more and
Nev-er did get up and walk_ the floor_ If this is love then

more and more_ and more._ You an - gel you_ You're as_

___ fine as _ can be_ The way you smile_ like a heav - en-ly child_ Is the

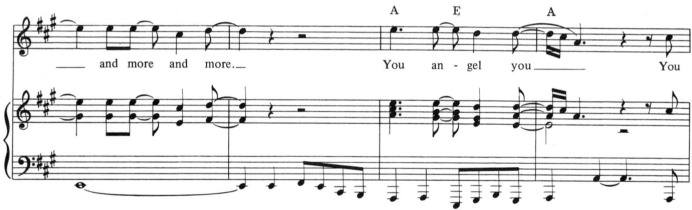

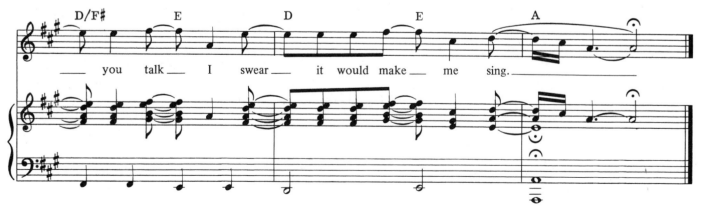

Nobody 'Cept You

WORDS AND MUSIC BY
BOB DYLAN

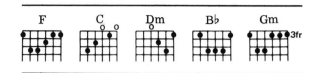

There's noth - ing ___ 'round here I be - lieve ___ in _____ 'Cept
Noth - ing 'round here I care to try ___ for _____ 'Cept

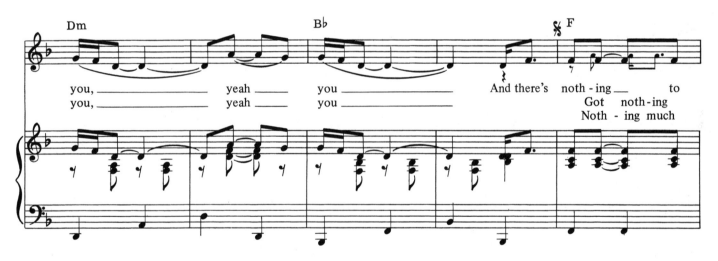

you, _____ yeah ____ you _____ And there's noth - ing ___ to
you, _____ yeah ____ you _____ Got noth - ing
Noth - ing much

me that's sa - cred _____ 'Cept you, _____ yeah you _____
left to live or die for _____ 'Cept you, _____ yeah you _____
mat - ters or seems to please me _____ 'Cept you, _____ yeah you _____

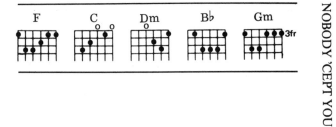

Used to play in the cem-e-ter-y Dance and sing and run when I was a

child _____ Nev-er seemed strange _____ But now I just__ pass

mourn-ful-ly__ by__ That place__ where the bones of life__ are piled _____

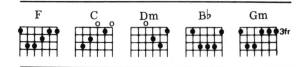

I know some-thin' has changed _____ I'm a stran-ger here _____ and no one

sees me _____ 'Cept you, _____ yeah ____ you _____

D. S. al Coda 𝄋

Coda

you _____

Tangled Up in Blue

WORDS AND MUSIC BY
BOB DYLAN

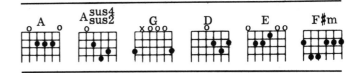

Moderately

1. Ear - ly one morn - in' the sun ___ was shin - in' I was lay - in' in bed ___

Won - d'rin' if ___ she'd changed at all ___ If her hair was ___ still

red. Her folks they said our lives ___ to - geth - er

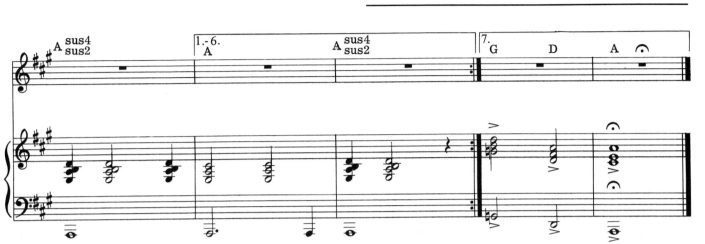

2.
```
A            |G              |
She was married when we first met
A            |G
Soon to be divorced
A            |G
I helped her out of a jam, I guess
   |D
But I used a little too much force
  |A          |G             |
We drove that car as far as we could
A            |G
Abandoned it out west
A            |G
Split up on a dark sad night
   |D              |
Both agreeing it was best
E            |F#m
She turned around to look at me
  |A        |D
As I was walkin' away
E            |F#m
I heard her say over my shoulder
   |A        |D
"We'll meet again some day
     |E      |
On the avenue"
```
G   D |A |A sus4 |A |A sus4 ||
                       sus2   sus2
Tangled up in blue

3.
```
A            |G                  |
I had a job in the great north woods
A            |G
Working as a cook for a spell
   |A        |G
But I never did like it all that much
   |D                |
And one day the axe just fell
   |A        |G
So I drifted down to New Orleans
   |A        |G            |
Where I happened to be employed
A            |G
Workin' for a while on a fishin' boat
   |D              |
Right outside of Delacroix
E            |F#m
But all the while I was alone
  |A        |D
The past was close behind
E            |F#m
I seen a lot of women
   |A        |D
But she never escaped my mind
   |E       |
And I just grew
```
G   D |A |A sus4 |A |A sus4 ||
                       sus2   sus2
Tangled up in blue

4.
```
A            |G              |
She was workin' in a topless place
  |A         |G
And I stopped in for a beer
 |A              |G
I just kept lookin' at the side of her face
   |D                |
In the spotlight so clear
   |A         |G
And later on as the crowd thinned out
  |A         |G
I's just about to do the same
A            |G
She was standing there in back of my chair
   |D            |              |
Said to me, "Don't I know your name?"
E            |F#m
I muttered somethin' underneath my breath
  |A         |G
She studied the lines on my face
 |E              |F#m
I must admit I felt a little uneasy
   |A         |D
When she bent down to tie the laces
     |E       |
Of my shoe
```
G   D |A |A sus4 |A |A sus4 ||
                       sus2   sus2
Tangled up in blue

5.
```
A            |G
She lit a burner on the stove
  |A         |G
And offered me a pipe
 |A              |G
"I thought you'd never say hello," she said
   |D        |
"You look like the silent type"
   |A         |G
Then she opened up a book of poems
   |A         |G   |
And handed it to me
A            |G
Written by an Italian poet
     |D           |
From the thirteenth century
  |E             |F#m
And every one of them words rang true
   |A         |D
And glowed like burnin' coal
E            |F#m
Pourin' off of every page
   |A        |D
Like it was written in my soul
   |E       |
From me to you
```
G   D |A |A sus4 |A |A sus4 ||
                       sus2   sus2
Tangled up in blue

6.
```
A            |G
I lived with them on Montague Street
A            |G
In a basement down the stairs
        |A         |G
There was music in the cafes at night
   |D        |
And revolution in the air
   |A         |G
Then he started into dealing with slaves
   |A         |G       |
And something inside of him died
A            |G
She had to sell everything she owned
   |D           |   |
And froze up inside
E            |F#m            |
And when finally the bottom fell out
A   |D
I became withdrawn
   |E         |F#m
The only thing I knew how to do
   |A        |D
Was to keep on keepin' on
   |E       |
Like a bird that flew
```
G   D |A |A sus4 |A |A sus4 ||
                       sus2   sus2
Tangled up in blue

7.
```
A            |G.
So now I'm goin' back again
A            |G
I got to get to her somehow
A            |G
All the people we used to know
         |D             |   |
They're an illusion to me now
A   |G
Some are mathematicians
A            |G
Some are carpenters' wives
   |D                  |
Don't know how it all got started
   |D                     |
I don't know what they're doin' with their lives
   |E         |F#m        |
But me, I'm still on the road
A        |D        |
Headin' for another joint
E            |F#m
We always did feel the same
   |A        |D
We just saw it from a different point
 |E     |   |
Of view
```
G   D |A |A sus4 |G   D |A ||
                       sus2
Tangled up in blue

If You See Her, Say Hello

WORDS AND MUSIC BY
BOB DYLAN

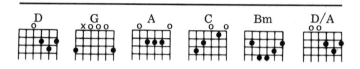

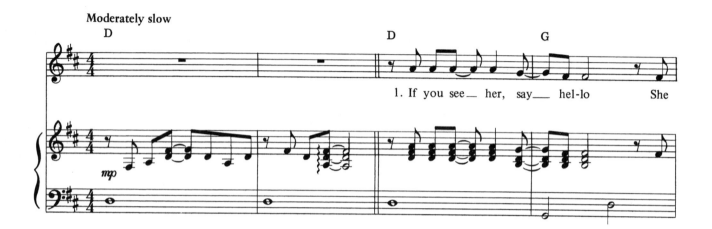

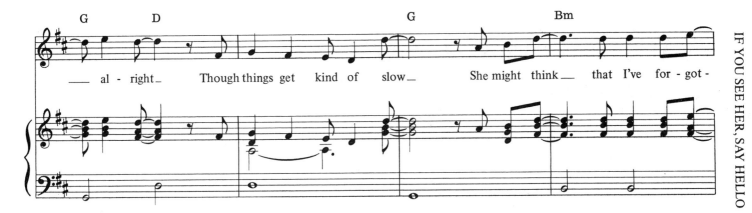

al - right __ Though things get kind of slow __ She might think __ that I've for - got -

ten her Don't tell her it is - n't so. __

2.
D |G   D
We had a fallin' out
  |A |D
Like lovers often will
            |G   D
And I to think of how she left that night
| |C |A
It still brings me a chill
    |Bm |G   D
And though our separation
| |C |A
It pierced me to the heart
Bm |D/A
She still lives inside of me
   |G |D | ||
We've never been apart

3.
D |G   D |
If you get close to her
A |D |
Kiss her once for me
         |G   D
I always have respected her
| |C |A |
For busting out and gettin' free
Bm |G   D
Oh whatever makes her happy
| |G
I won't stand in the way
   |Bm |D/A
Though the bitter taste still lingers on
    |G |D | ||
From the night I tried to make her stay

4.
D |G   D |
I see a lot of people
A |D
As I make the rounds
| |G   D
And I hear her name here and there
| |C |A
As I go from town to town
   |Bm |G   D
And I've never gotten used to it
| |G
I've just learned to turn it off
Bm |D/A
Either I'm too sensitive
   |G |D | ||
Or else I'm gettin' soft

5.
D |G   D |
Sundown, yellow moon
A |D |
I replay the past
         |G   D
I know every scene by heart
| |C |A |
They all went by so fast
Bm |G   D
If she's passin' back this way
| |G
I'm not that hard to find
Bm |D/A |
Tell her she can look me up
G |D | ||
If she's got the time

You're Gonna Make Me Lonesome When You Go

WORDS AND MUSIC BY

BOB DYLAN

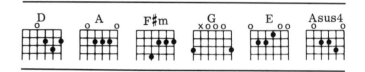

I've seen love go by my door __ It's nev - er been __ this
Drag - on clouds so high a - bove __ I've on - ly known __ this
Pur - ple clo - ver, Queen Anne lace __ Crim - son hair __ a -

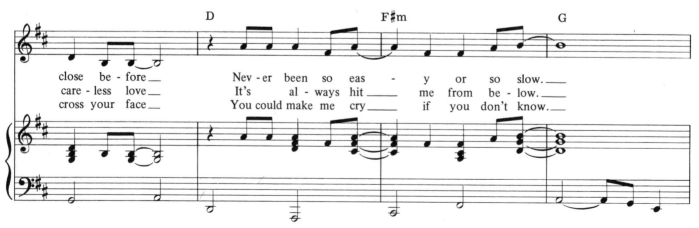

close be - fore __ Nev - er been so eas - y or so slow. __
care - less love __ It's al - ways hit __ me from be - low. __
cross your face __ You could make me cry __ if you don't know. __

Been shoot-ing in ____ the dark too long ____ When
This time a - round it's more cor - rect ____
Can't re - mem - ber what I was think - in' of You

some - thin's not right it's wrong Yer gon - na make me lone -
Right on tar - get, so di - rect Yer gon - na make me lone -
might be spoil - in' me too much, love Yer gon - na make me lone -

some ___ when you go.
some ___ when you go.
some ___ when you go.

Flow - ers on the hill - side, bloom-in' cra - zy ____
Yer gon - na make me won - der what I'm do - in' ____

Crick - ets talk - in' back ___ and forth ___ in rhyme
Stay - in' far be - hind ___ with - out ___ you

Blue riv - er run - nin' slow and la - zy
Yer gon - na make me won - der what I'm say - in'

I could stay with you for - ev - er And nev - er re - al - ize the time. I'll
Yer gon - na make me give my - self ___ a good talk - in' to.

Sit - u - a - tions have end - ed sad ___ Re - la - tion - ships ___ have all ___
look for you ___ in old Hon - o - lu - lu San Fran - cis - co, Ash -

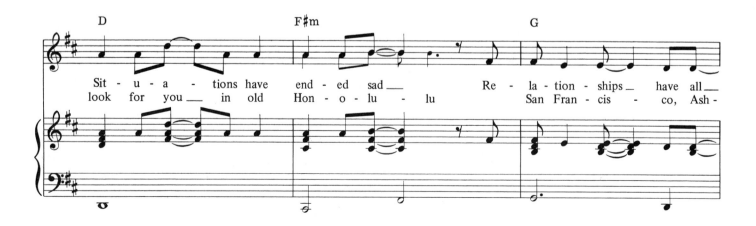

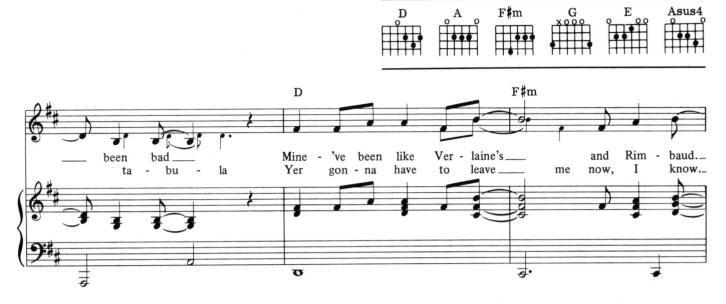

been bad ___
ta - bu - la

Mine - 've been like Ver - laine's ___ and Rim - baud.
Yer gon - na have to leave ___ me now, I know. ___

___
___

But there's no way I can ___ com - pare ___
But I'll see you way in the sky ___ a - bove ___ In the

All those scenes ___ to this af - fair
tall grass ___ in the ones I love ___

Yer gon - na make me lone -
Yer gon - na make me lone -

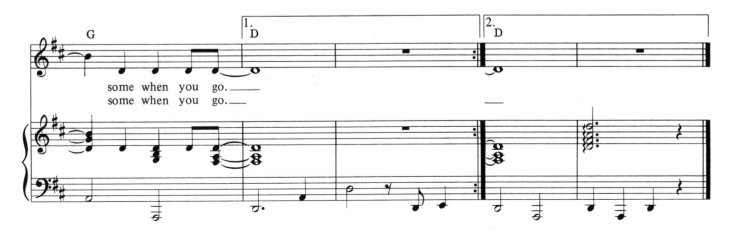

some when you go. ___
some when you go. ___

Lily, Rosemary and the Jack of Hearts

WORDS AND MUSIC BY

BOB DYLAN

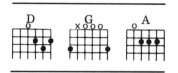

Fast Country style

1. The fes - ti - val __ was o - ver The boys were all

plan - nin' for a fall __

The cab - a - ret __ was qui - et Ex - cept for the

drill - in' in the wall __

The cur-few had been lift-ed And the gam-blin' wheel shut down An-y-one with an-y sense Had al-read-y left town He was stand-in' in the door-way Look-in' like the Jack of Hearts.

1.–15.

16. *D.S. (Instrumental) and fade*

2. He

2.
D | |
He moved across the mirrored room
G | |D | |
"Set it up for everyone," he said
| |
Then everyone commenced to do
|G | |D | | |
What they were doin' before he turned their heads
|G |D
Then he walked up to a stranger
|A |D
And he asked him with a grin
|G |D
"Could you kindly tell me, friend
|A |
What time the show begins?"
|D | |
Then he moved into the corner
G |A |D | | | ||
Face down like the Jack of Hearts

3.
D | |
Backstage the girls were playin'
G | |D | | |
Five card stud by the stairs
| |
Lily had two queens
|G | |D | | | |
She was hopin' for a third to match her pair
G |D
Outside, the streets were fillin' up
|A |D
The window was open wide
|G |D
A gentle breeze was blowin'
|A | |
You could feel it from inside
D | |
Lily called another bet
G |A |D | | | ||
And drew up the Jack of Hearts

4.
D |
Big Jim was no one's fool
|G | |D | | |
He owned the town's only diamond mine
| |
He made his usual entrance
G | |D | | |
Lookin' so dandy and so fine
|G |D
With his bodyguards and silver cane
|A |D
And every hair in place
|G |D
He took whatever he wanted to
|A
And he laid it all to waste
|D
But his bodyguards and silver cane
|G |A |D | | | ||
Were no match for the Jack of Hearts

5.
D |
Rosemary combed her hair
|G | |D | | |
And took a carriage into town
| | |
She slipped in through the side door
G | |D | | |
Lookin' like a queen without a crown
|G |D
She fluttered her false eyelashes
|A |D
And whispered in his ear
G |D
"Sorry, darlin', that I'm late"
|A |
But he didn't seem to hear
|D | |
He was starin' into space
G |A |D | | | ||
Over at the Jack of Hearts

6.
D | |
"I know I've seen that face somewhere,"
G | |D | | |
Big Jim was thinkin' to himself
| |
"Maybe down in Mexico
|G | |D | | |
Or a picture up on somebody's shelf"
|G |D
But then the crowd began to stamp their feet
|A |D
And the house lights did dim
|G |D
And in the darkness of the room
|A | |
There was only Jim and him
D | |
Starin' at the butterfly
|G |A |D | | | ||
Who just drew the Jack of Hearts

7.
D |
Lily was a princess
|G | |D | | |
She was fair-skinned and precious as a child
| |
She did whatever she had to do
|G | |D | | |
She had that certain flash everytime she smiled
|G |D
She'd come away from a broken home
|A |D
Had lots of strange affairs
|G |D
With men in every walk of life
|A |
Which took her everywhere
|D | |
But she'd never met anyone
G |A |D | | | ||
Quite like the Jack of Hearts

8.
D | |
The hangin' judge came in
G | |D | | |
Unnoticed and was being wined and dined
| |
The drillin' in the wall kept up
|G | |D | | |
But no one seemed to pay it any mind
|G |D
It was known all around
|A |D
That Lily had Jim's ring
|G |D |
And nothing would ever come between
A |
Lily and the king
|D |
No, nothin' ever would
G |A |D | | | ||
Except maybe the Jack of Hearts

9.
D |
Rosemary started drinkin' hard
|G | |D | | |
And seein' her reflection in the knife
| | |
She was tired of the attention
G | |D | | |
Tired of playin' the role of Big Jim's wife
|G |D
She had done a lot of bad things
|A |D
Even once tried suicide
|G |D |
Was lookin' to do just one good deed
A |
Before she died
|D | |
She was gazin' to the future
G |A |D | | | ||
Riding on the Jack of Hearts

D |
| G | D | A |

10.   Lily washed her face, took her dress off and
G | |D | |
Buried it away
"Has your luck run out," she laughed at him
   |G | |D | |
"Well, I guess you must have known it would someday
   |G |D
Be careful not to touch the wall
       |A |D
There's a brand-new coat of paint
    |G |D
I'm glad to see you're still alive
     |A | |
You're lookin' like a saint"
D |
Down the hallway footsteps
  |G |A |D | | ||
Were comin' for the Jack of Hearts

D |
11.   The backstage manager
  |G | |D | |
Was pacing all around by his chair
"There's something funny going on,"
  |G | |D | |
He said, "I can just feel it in the air"
  |G |D
He went to get the hangin' judge
But the hangin' judge was drunk
   |G |D
As the leading actor hurried by
   |A |
In the costume of a monk
There was no actor anywhere
G |A |D | | | ||
Better than the Jack of Hearts

D |
12.   Lily's arms were locked around
  |G | |D | |
The man that she dearly loved to touch
She forgot all about
  |G | |D | |
The man she couldn't stand who hounded her so much
  |G |D
"I've missed you so," she said to him
And he felt she was sincere
  |G |D
But just beyond the door
   |A | |
He felt jealousy and fear
D |
Just another night
  |G |A |D | | | ||
In the life of the Jack of Hearts

D |
13.   No one knew the circumstance
  |G | |D | | |
But they say that it happened pretty quick
The door to the dressing room
   |G | |D | |
Burst open and a cold revolver clicked
  |G |D
And Big Jim was standin' there
  |A |D |
Ya couldn't say surprised
G |D |
Rosemary right beside him
A |
Steady in her eyes
   |D |
She was with Big Jim
    |G |A |D | | | ||
But she was leanin' to the Jack of Hearts

D | |G |
14.   Two doors down the boys finally made it
      |D | |
Through the wall
And cleaned out the bank safe
  |G | |D | |
It's said that they got off with quite a haul
  |G |D
In the darkness by the river bed
  |A |D
They waited on the ground
  |G |D
For one more member
   |A |
Who had business back in town
   |D |
But they couldn't go no further
G |A |D | | | ||
Without the Jack of Hearts

D |
15.   The next day was hangin' day
  |G | |D | |
The sky was overcast and black
Big Jim lay covered up
G | |D | |
Killed by a penknife in the back
  |G |D
And Rosemary on the gallows
  |A |D
She didn't even blink
  |G |D
The hangin' judge was sober
  |A |
He hadn't had a drink
  |D |
The only person on the scene
G |A |D | | | ||
Missin' was the Jack of Hearts

D |
16.   The cabaret was empty now
  |G | |D | | |
A sign said, "Closed for repair"
Lily had already taken
G | |D | |
All of the dye out of her hair
  |G |D
She was thinkin' 'bout her father
  |A |D
Who she very rarely saw
G |D
Thinkin' 'bout Rosemary
  |A |
And thinkin' about the law
  |D |
But most of all
  |G |A |D | | | ||
She was thinkin' 'bout the Jack of Hearts

Shelter from the Storm

WORDS AND MUSIC BY
BOB DYLAN

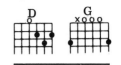

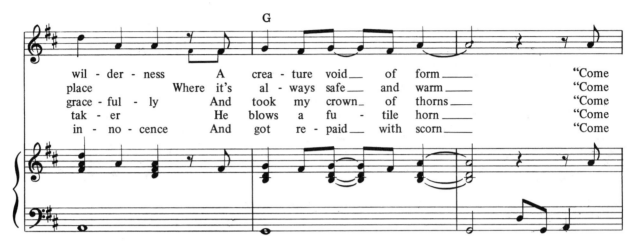

wil - der - ness   A   crea - ture void___ of   form___   "Come
place   Where it's   al - ways safe___ and   warm___   "Come
grace - ful - ly   And   took   my   crown_ of   thorns___   "Come
tak - er   He   blows   a   fu - tile   horn___   "Come
in - no - cence   And   got   re - paid__ with   scorn___   "Come

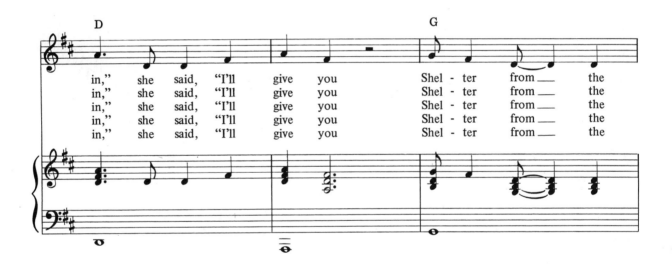

in,"   she   said,   "I'll   give   you   Shel - ter   from ___ the
in,"   she   said,   "I'll   give   you   Shel - ter   from ___ the
in,"   she   said,   "I'll   give   you   Shel - ter   from ___ the
in,"   she   said,   "I'll   give   you   Shel - ter   from ___ the
in,"   she   said,   "I'll   give   you   Shel - ter   from ___ the

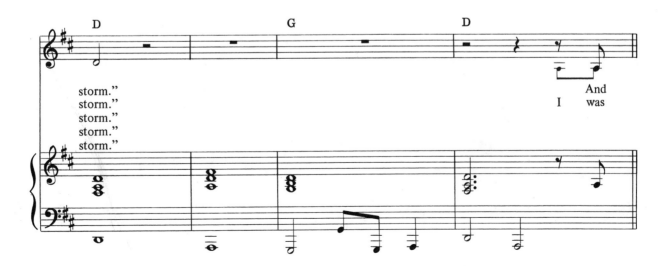

storm."
storm."   And
storm."   I   was
storm."
storm."

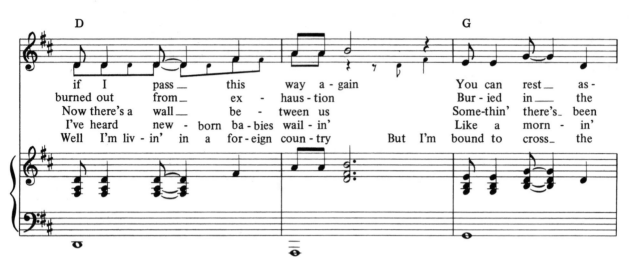

if I   pass___   this   way a - gain   You can   rest___   as -
burned out   from___   ex - haus - tion   Bur - ied   in ___   the
Now there's a   wall___   be - tween us   Some-thin'   there's___   been
I've heard   new - born ba - bies wail - in'   Like a   morn - in'
Well   I'm liv - in'   in a   for - eign coun - try   But I'm   bound to   cross___   the

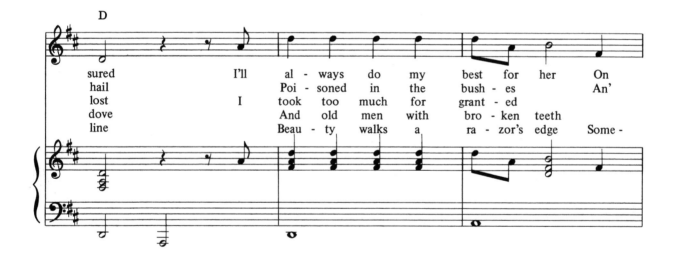

sured   I'll   al - ways   do   my   best   for her   On
hail   Poi - soned   in   the   bush - es   An'
lost   I   took   too   much   for   grant - ed
dove   And   old   men   with   bro - ken teeth
line   Beau - ty   walks   a   ra - zor's edge   Some -

that   I   give___   my   word.   In   a   world   of   steel - eyed
blown out   on ___   the   trail.   Hunt - ed   like   a
Got my   sig - nals   crossed.   Just   to   think   that   it
Strand - ed   with - out   love.   Do   I   un - der - stand   your
day   I'll   make___   it   mine.   If   I   could   on - ly   turn

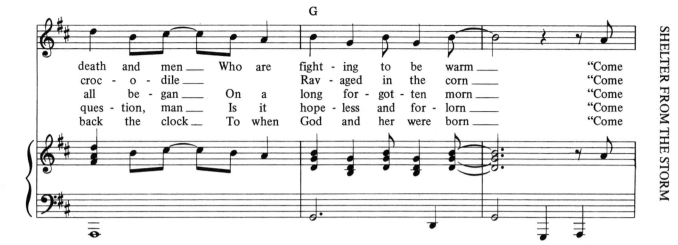

death and men ___ Who are fight - ing to be warm ___ "Come
croc - o - dile ___ Rav - aged in the corn ___ "Come
all be - gan ___ On a long for - got - ten morn ___ "Come
ques - tion, man ___ Is it hope - less and for - lorn ___ "Come
back the clock ___ To when God and her were born ___ "Come

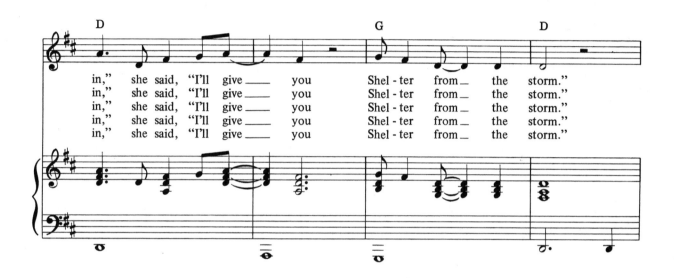

in," she said, "I'll give ___ you Shel - ter from ___ the storm."
in," she said, "I'll give ___ you Shel - ter from ___ the storm."
in," she said, "I'll give ___ you Shel - ter from ___ the storm."
in," she said, "I'll give ___ you Shel - ter from ___ the storm."
in," she said, "I'll give ___ you Shel - ter from ___ the storm."

Not a
Sud - den -
Well the
In a

Idiot Wind

WORDS AND MUSIC BY

BOB DYLAN

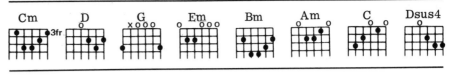

2.
```
Cm                   |
I ran into the fortune teller
  | D            |              | G       |   |
Who said beware of lightning that might strike
Cm               |            |
I haven't known peace and quiet
D            |              | G            |
For so long I can't remember what it's like
       | Em        | Bm       |
There's a lone soldier on the cross
Am              | G            |
Smoke pourin' out of a box-car door
Em          | Bm
You didn't know it, you didn't think it could be done
     | Am        | G
In the final end he won the war
     | Bm        | C      |   |
After losin' every battle
Cm           |              |
I woke up on the roadside
D            |                     | G    |   |
Daydreamin' 'bout the way things sometimes are
Cm              |            |
Visions of your chestnut mare
D            |                | G       |
Shoot through my head and are makin' me see stars
       | Em        | Bm       |
You hurt the ones that I love best
    | Am        | G            |
And cover up the truth with lies
Em          | Bm            |
One day you'll be in the ditch
Am       | G            |
Flies buzzin' around your eyes
Bm        | C       |    ||
Blood on your saddle

G   |         |
Idiot wind
C            |              | G       |   |
Blowing through the flowers on your tomb
C            |              | D sus 4  | D    |
Blowing through the curtains in your room
G   |         |
Idiot wind
C            |              | G       |
Blowing every time ya move your teeth
        |    | C
You're an idiot, babe
    | D            |              | G       ||
It's a wonder that you still know how to breathe
```

3.
```
Cm                   |
It was gravity which pulled us down
  | D            |              | G       |   |
And destiny which broke us apart
Cm               |            |
You tamed the lion in my cage
D            |                   | G            |
But it just wasn't enough to change my heart
       | Em        | Bm       |
Now everything's a little upside down
    | Am        | G            |
As a matter of fact the wheels have stopped
Em          | Bm
What's good is bad, what's bad is good
     | Am        | G
You'll find out when you reach the top
     | Bm    | C      |   |
You're on the bottom
Cm           |              |
I noticed at the ceremony
  | D            |              | G    |   |
Your corrupt ways had finally made you blind
Cm              |            |
I can't remember your face anymore
D            |                | G       |
Your mouth is changed, your eyes don't look into mine
       | Em        | Bm       |
The priest wore black on the seventh day
    | Am        | G            |
And sat stone-faced while the building burned
| Em          | Bm            |
I waited for you on the running boards
     | Am            | G            |
Near the cypress tree while the springtime turned
Bm        | C       |    ||
Slowly into autumn

G   |         |
Idiot wind
C            |              | G       |
Blowing like a circle around my skull
             | C      |                    | D sus 4    | D    |
From the Grand Coulee Dam to the Capitol
G   |         |
Idiot wind
C            |              | G       |
Blowing every time you move your teeth
        |    | C
You're an idiot, babe
    | D            |              | G       ||
It's a wonder that you still know how to breathe
```

4.
```
Cm             |              |
I can't feel you anymore
D            |              | G       |   |
I can't even touch the books you've read
Cm               |
Everytime I crawl past your door
  | D            |              | G       |   |
I been wishin' I was somebody else instead
Em          | Bm            |
Down the highway, down the tracks
Am          | G            |
Down the road to ecstasy
Em          | Bm
I followed you beneath the stars
Am          | G
Hounded by your memory
  | Bm        | C       |   |
And all your ragin' glory
Cm               |
I been double-crossed now
     | D            |              | G    |   |
For the very last time and now I'm finally free
Cm           |              |
I kissed goodbye the howling beast
D            |                   | G    |   |
On the borderline which separated you  from me
Em          | Bm            |
You'll never know the hurt I suffered
```

```
Am          | G
Nor the pain I rise above
  | Em        | Bm
And I'll never know the same about you
    | Am        | G
Your holiness or your kind of love
       | Bm
And it makes me feel
  | C       |    ||
So sorry

G   |         |
Idiot wind
C            |              | G       |   |
Blowing through the buttons of our coats
C            |              | D sus 4  | D    |
Blowing through the letters that we wrote
G   |         |
Idiot wind
C            |              | G       |
Blowing through the dust upon our shelves
        |    | C
We're idiots, babe
    | D            |              | G       ||
It's a wonder we can even feed ourselves
```

Meet Me in the Morning

WORDS AND MUSIC BY
BOB DYLAN

Slow Blues

1. Meet me in the morn-ing Fif-ty-Sixth and Wa-ba-sha

Meet me in the morn-ing Fif-ty-Sixth and Wa-ba-sha

Hon-ey we could be in Kan-sas

By time the snow be-gins to thaw.

2. D
Is right before the dawn
G7 |D | |
They say the darkest hour
G7
They say the darkest hour
|D
Is right before the dawn
|A7 |
But you wouldn't know it by me
G7 |D | ||
Every day's been darkness since you been gone

3. D
Little rooster crowin'
G7 |D | |
There must be something on his mind
G7 |
Little rooster crowin'

There must be something on his mind |D |
|A7 |
Well I feel just like that rooster
G7 |D | ||
Honey ya treat me so unkind

4. D
The birds are flying low, babe
G7 |D | |
Honey I feel so exposed
G7
Well the birds are flying low, babe
|D |
Honey I feel so exposed
|A7 |
Well now I ain't got any matches
G |D | ||
And the station doors are closed

5. D
Well I struggled through barbed wire
G7 |D | |
Felt the hail fall from above
G7
Well I struggled through barbed wire
|D |
Felt the hail fall from above
|A7 |
Well you know I even outran the hound dogs
G7 |D | ||
Honey you know I've earned your love

6. D
Look at the sun
G7 |D | |
Sinkin' like a ship
G7
Look at the sun
|D | |
Sinkin' like a ship
A7 |
Ain't that just like my heart, babe
G7 |D | D7 ||
When you kissed my lips

Buckets of Rain

WORDS AND MUSIC BY
BOB DYLAN

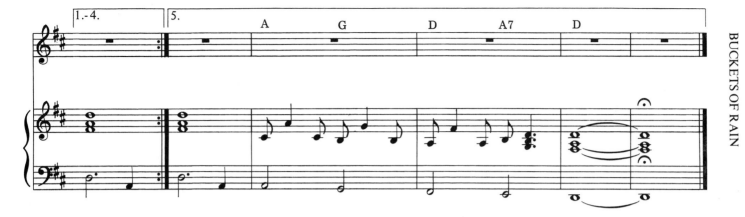

2.
D sus 2 / sus 4 D | D sus 2 / sus 4 D
I been meek and hard like an oak

|D sus 2 / sus 4 D | D sus 2 / sus 4 D |
I seen pretty people disappear like smoke

G |
Friends will arrive

|D |
Friends will disappear

|A G |
If you want me

D A7 |D | ||
Honey baby, I'll be here

3.
D sus 2 / sus 4 D | D sus 2 / sus 4 D |
Like your smile and your fingertips

D sus 2 / sus 4 D | D sus 2 / sus 4 D
Like the way that you move your lips

|G |
I like the cool way

|D | |
You look at me

A G
Everything about you

|D A7 |D | ||
Is bringing me misery

4.
D sus 2 / sus 4 D | D sus 2 / sus 4 D
Little red wagon, little red bike

|D sus 2 / sus 4 D | D sus 2 / sus 4 D
I ain't no monkey but I know what I like

|G |
I like the way you love me

|D |
Strong and slow

|A G |
I'm takin' you with me

D A7 |D | ||
Honey baby, when I go

5.
D sus 2 / sus 4 D | D sus 2 / sus 4 D |
Life is sad, life is a bust

D sus 2 / sus 4 D | D sus 2 / sus 4 D
All ya can do is do what you must

|G |
You do what you must do

|D |
And ya do it well

|A G |
I'll do it for you

D A7 |D | |A G|D A7|D | ||
Honey baby, can't you tell

You're a Big Girl Now

WORDS AND MUSIC BY
BOB DYLAN

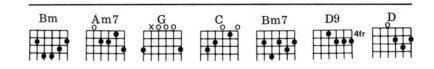

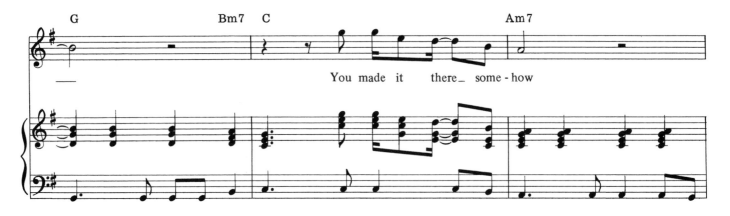

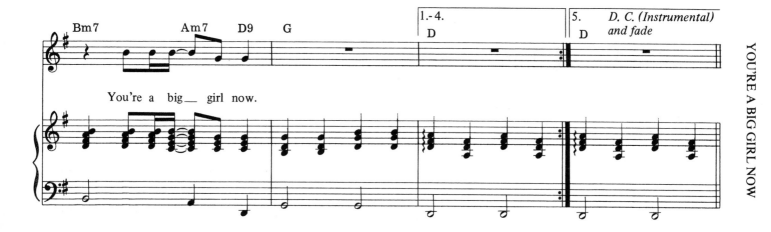

You're a big___ girl now.

2.
Bm
Bird on the horizon
Am7
Sittin' on a fence
Bm
He's singin' his song for me
Am7
At his own expense
|G
And I'm just like that bird
|C
Oh – oh
|G Bm7|C
Singin' just for you
|Am7
I hope that you can hear
Bm7 Am7 D9 |G |D ||
Hear me singin' through these tears

3.
Bm
Time is a jet plane
Am7
It moves too fast
Bm
Oh, but what a shame
|Am7
If all we've shared can't last
|G
I can change, I swear
|C
Oh – oh
|G Bm7|C
See what you can do
|Am7
I can make it through
Bm7 Am7 D9 |G |D ||
You can make it too

4.
Bm
Love is so simple
Am7
To quote a phrase
Bm
You've known it all the time
Am7
I'm learnin' it these days
|G
Oh, I know where I can find you
|C
Oh – oh
|G Bm7|C
In somebody's room
|Am7
It's a price I have to pay
Bm7 Am7 D9 | G |D ||
You're a big girl all the way

5.
Bm
A change in the weather
Am7
Is known to be extreme
Bm
But what's the sense of changing
Am7
Horses in midstream
|G
I'm going out of my mind
|C
Oh – oh
|G Bm7|C
With a pain that stops and starts
|Am7
Like a corkscrew to my heart
Bm7 Am7 D9 |G |D || D.C. (Instrumental) and fade
Ever since we've been apart

Simple Twist of Fate

WORDS AND MUSIC BY
BOB DYLAN

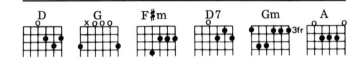

They sat to-geth-er in the park
A sax-o-phone some-place far off played
He hears the tick-ing of the clocks

As the eve-ning sky____ grew dark
As she was walk-in' by the ar-cade
And walks a-long with a par-rot that talks

She looked at him and he felt a
As the light bust through a beat-up
Hunts her down by the wa-ter-front

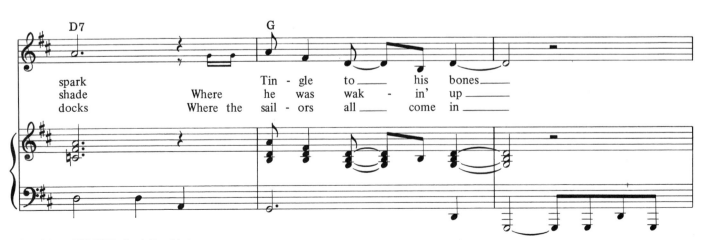

spark
shade
docks

Tin-gle to____ his bones____
Where he was wak-in' up ____
Where the sail-ors all____ come in ____

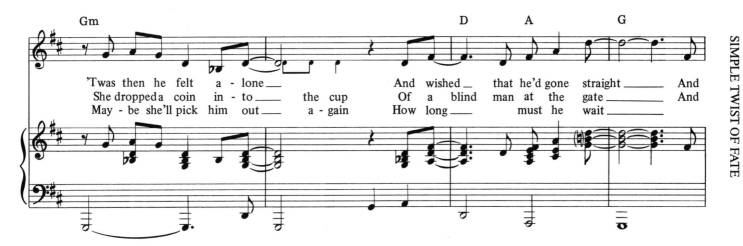

'Twas then he felt a - lone___ And wished___ that he'd gone straight___ And
She dropped a coin in - to___ the cup Of a blind man at the gate_____ And
May - be she'll pick him out___ a - gain How long___ must he wait_____

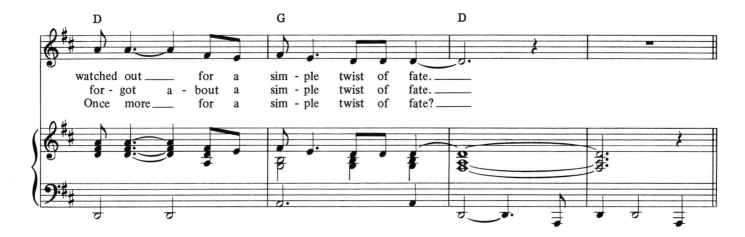

watched out___ for a sim - ple twist of fate.___
for - got a - bout a sim - ple twist of fate.___
Once more___ for a sim - ple twist of fate?___

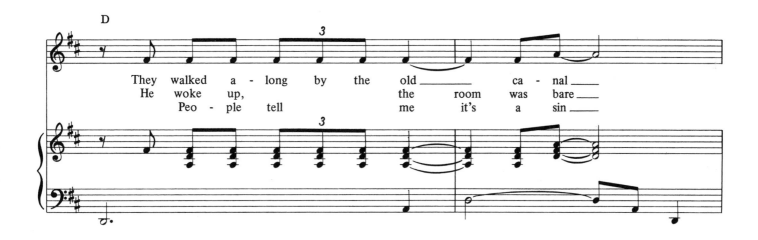

They walked a - long by the old___ ca - nal___
He woke up, the room was bare___
Peo - ple tell me it's a sin___

A lit - tle con - fused I re - mem - ber well
He did - n't see her an - y - where
To know and feel too much with - in

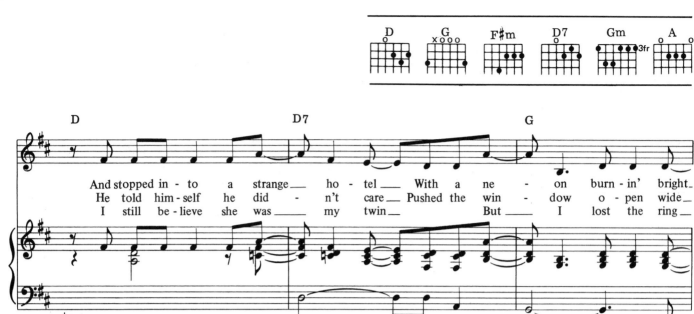

Up to Me

WORDS AND MUSIC BY
BOB DYLAN

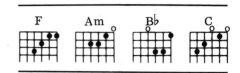

Moderately fast

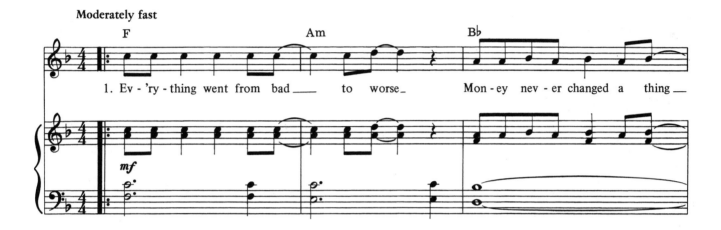

1. Ev - 'ry-thing went from bad ___ to worse ___ Mon - ey nev - er changed a thing ___

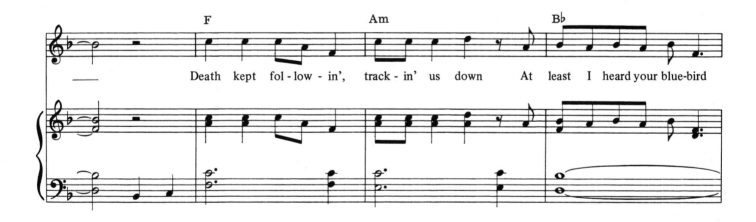

___ Death kept fol - low - in', track - in' us down At least I heard your blue-bird

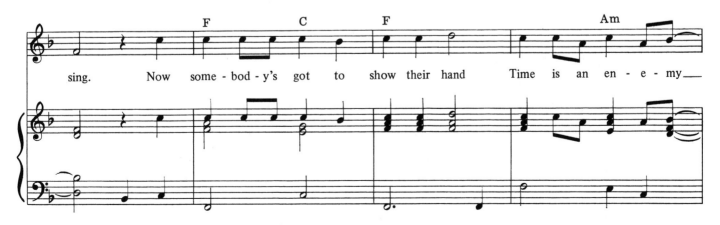

sing. Now some - bod - y's got to show their hand Time is an en - e - my ___

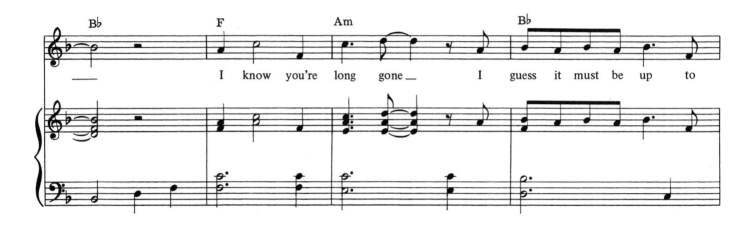

I know you're long gone ___ I guess it must be up to

me.

2. If I'd of me.

2.

N.C. ‖ F | Am
If I'd of thought about it I never would've done it
| Bb |
I guess I would-a let it slide
| F | Am
If I'd-a lived my life by what others were thinkin'
| Bb |
The heart inside me would-a died
| F C | F
I was just too stubborn to ever be governed
| F Am | Bb |
By enforced insanity
F | Am
Someone had to reach for the risin' star
| Bb | F | F C | F | Bb
I guess it was up to me

3.
N.C. ‖ F | Am
Oh, the Union Central is pullin' out
| Bb |
And the orchids are in bloom
| F | Am
I've only got me one good shirt left
| Bb |
And it smells of stale perfume
| F C | F
In fourteen months I've only smiled once
| F Am | Bb |
And I didn't do it consciously
F | Am
Somebody's got to find your trail
| Bb | F | F C | F | Bb
I guess it must be up to me

4.
N.C. ‖ F | Am
It was like a revelation
| Bb |
When you betrayed me with your touch
| F | Am
I'd just about convinced myself
| Bb |
That nothin' had changed that much
| F C | F
The old Rounder in the iron mask
F Am | Bb |
Slipped me the master key
F | Am
Somebody had to unlock your heart
| Bb | F | F C | F | Bb
He said it was up to me

5.
N.C. ‖ F | Am |
Well, I watched you slowly disappear
Bb |
Down into the officers' club
| F | Am
I would've followed you in the door
| Bb |
But I didn't have a ticket stub
| F C | F
So I waited all night 'til the break of day
| F Am | Bb |
Hopin' one of us could get free
| F | Am
When the dawn came over the river bridge
| Bb | F | F C | F | Bb
I knew it was up to me

6.
```
N.C.  ‖ F            | A m
```
Oh, the only decent thing I did
```
       | B b                |
```
When I worked as a postal clerk
```
       | F            | A m
```
Was to haul your picture down off the wall
```
       | B b                    |
```
Near the cage where I used to work
```
       | F  C      | F
```
Was I a fool or not to try
```
       | F        A m       | B b
```
To protect your identity
```
       | F            | A m
```
You looked a little burned out, my friend
```
   | B b                | F    | F  C   | F   | B b
```
I thought it might be up to me

7.
```
N.C.  ‖ F            | A m
```
Well, I met somebody face to face
```
       | B b                |
```
And I had to remove my hat
```
       | F       | A m
```
She's everything I need and love
```
       | B b                |
```
But I can't be swayed by that
```
       | F     C    | F .
```
It frightens me, the awful truth
```
       | F      A m   | B b
```
Of how sweet life can be
```
       | F            | A m
```
But she ain't a-gonna make a move
```
   | B b                | F    | F  C   | F   | B b
```
I guess it must be up to me

8.
```
N.C.  ‖ F            | A m
```
We heard the Sermon on the Mount
```
       | B b                |
```
And I knew it was too complex
```
       | F       | A m
```
It didn't amount to anything more
```
       | B b                    |
```
Than what the broken glass reflects
```
       | F     C    | F
```
When you bite off more than you can chew
```
       | F      A m    | B b   |
```
You pay the penalty
```
   F            | A m
```
Somebody's got to tell the tale
```
   | B b                | F    | F  C   | F   | B b
```
I guess it must be up to me

9.
```
N.C.  ‖ F            | A m
```
Well, Dupree came in pimpin' tonight
```
       | B b                |  |
```
To the Thunderbird Cafe
```
   F            | A m
```
Crystal wanted to talk to him
```
       | B b                |
```
I had to look the other way
```
       | F        c      | F            |
```
Well, I just can't rest without you, love
```
   F        A m       | B b
```
I need your company
```
       | F            | A m
```
But you ain't a-gonna cross the line
```
   | B b                | F    | F  C   | F   | B b
```
I guess it must be up to me

10.
```
N.C.  ‖ F            | A m
```
There's a note left in the bottle
```
       | B b                |  |
```
You can give it to Estelle
```
   F            | A m
```
She's the one you been wondrin' about
```
       | B b                    |
```
But there's really nothin' much to tell
```
       | F     C    | F
```
We both heard voices for awhile
```
       | F      A m   | B b   |
```
Now the rest is history
```
   F            | A m
```
Somebody's got to cry some tears
```
   | B b                | F    | F  C   | F   | B b
```
I guess it must be up to me

11.
```
N.C.  ‖ F            | A m            |
```
So go on boys and play your hands
```
   B b                |
```
Life is a pantomime
```
       | F            | A m
```
The ringleaders from the county seat
```
       | B b                    |
```
Say you don't have all that much time
```
       | F     C    | F
```
And the girl with me behind the shades
```
       | F        A m       | B b   |
```
She ain't my property
```
   F            | A m
```
One of us has got to hit the road
```
   | B b                | F    | F  C   | F   | B b
```
I guess it must be up to me

12.
```
N.C.  ‖ F        | A m            |
```
And if we never meet again
```
   B b                |
```
Baby remember me
```
       | F            | A m
```
How my lone guitar played sweet for you
```
       | B b                |
```
That old-time melody
```
       | F     C | F
```
And the harmonica around my neck
```
   | F        A m       | B b   |
```
I blew it for you, free
```
   F            | A m
```
No one else could play that tune
```
       | B b                | F    ‖
```
You know it was up to me

I Shall Be Released

WORDS AND MUSIC BY

BOB DYLAN

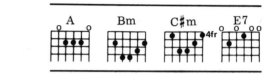

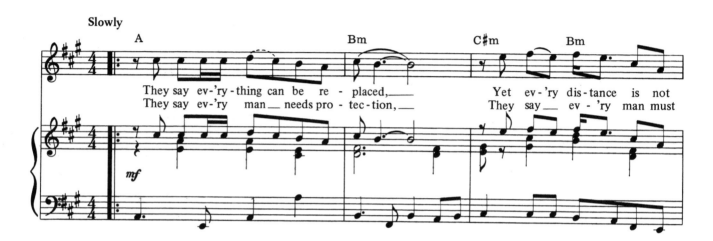

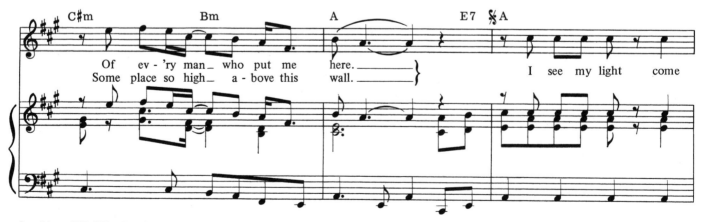

Lyrics:

They say ev-'ry-thing can be re-placed,____ Yet ev-'ry dis-tance is not near.____ So I re-mem-ber ev-'ry face____ Of ev-'ry man_ who put me here.____ I see my light come

They say ev-'ry man_ needs pro-tec-tion,____ They say_ ev-'ry man must fall.____ Yet I swear I_ see my re-flec-tion Some place so high_ a-bove this wall.____

shin - ing From the west__ un - to the east.__

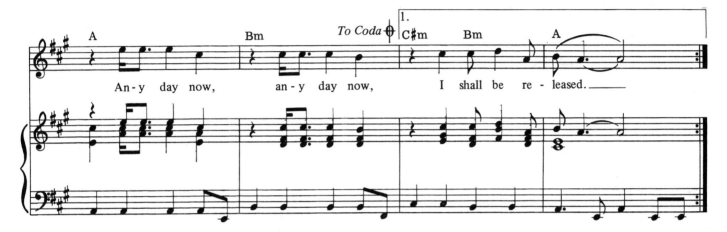

An - y day now, an - y day now, I shall be re - leased.__

I shall be re - leased.__ Stand - ing next to me in this lone - ly

crowd,__ Is a man who swears he's not to blame.__

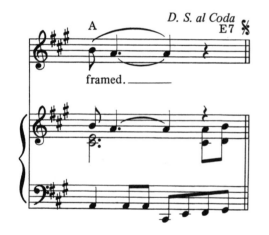

All day long I hear him shout ____ so loud, Cry-ing out ____ that he was

framed. ____

I shall be re - leased. ____

Odds and Ends

WORDS AND MUSIC BY
BOB DYLAN

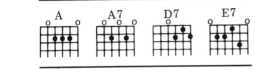

Moderately slow Rock Blues

plan it all___ and I take my place___
take your file___ and you bend my head___

You break your prom - ise all
I nev-er can re - mem-ber an - y -

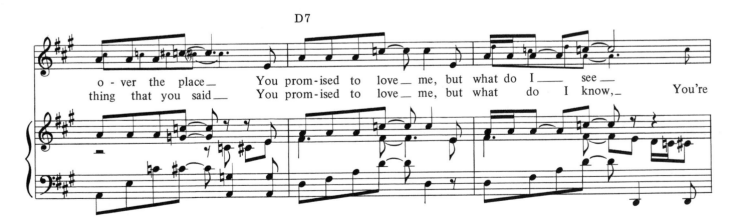

o - ver the place___ You prom-ised to love___ me, but what do I____ see
thing that you said___ You prom-ised to love___ me, but what do I know,___ You're

Just you com - in'_____ and spill - in' juice o - ver me
al - ways spill - in' juice on me like you got some place to go

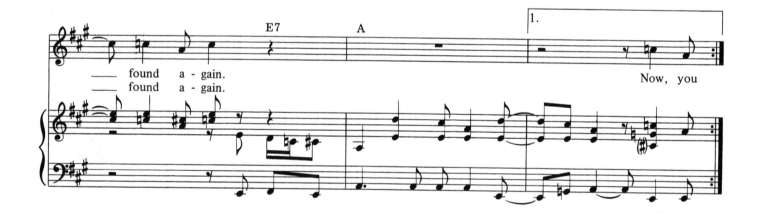

Odds and ends,___ odds and ends ___ Lost time is not ___
Odds and ends,___ odds and ends ___ Lost time is not ___

_____ found a - gain.
_____ found a - gain.

Now, you

Now, I've had e - nough,_ my box is clean ___ You

know what I'm say-in'___ and you know what I mean ___ From now on ___ you'd

best get on some-one else While you're do-in' it, ___ keep that juice to your-self ___

Odds and ends, ___ odds and ends ___ Lost time is not ___

___ found a-gain.

Million Dollar Bash

WORDS AND MUSIC BY
BOB DYLAN

Moderately

1. Well, that big dumb blonde With her wheel in the gorge __ And

Tur - tle, that friend of theirs With his checks all forged __ And his cheeks in a chunk With his

cheese in the cash They're all gon - na be there At that mil - lion dol - lar bash.

Ooh, ba - by, ooh - ee __ Ooh, ba - by,

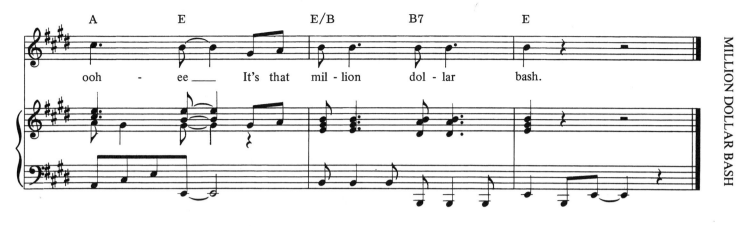

ooh - ee ____ It's that mil - lion dol - lar bash.

2. E
Ev'rybody from right now
| A
To over there and back
| E
The louder they come
| B7 |
The harder they crack
E |
Come now, sweet cream
A
Don't forget to flash
| E
We're all gonna meet
| B7   E |
At that million dollar bash
C#m | A   E |
Ooh, baby, ooh-ee
C#m | A   E
Ooh, baby, ooh-ee
| E/B   B7 | E ||
It's that million dollar bash

3. E |
Well, I took my counselor
A
Out to the barn
| E
Silly Nelly was there
| B7
She told him a yarn
| E |
Then along came Jones
A |
Emptied the trash
E
Ev'rybody went down
| B7   E |
To that million dollar bash
C#m | A   E |
Ooh, baby, ooh-ee
C#m | A   E
Ooh, baby, ooh-ee
| E/B   B7 | E ||
It's that million dollar bash

4. E
Well, I'm hittin' it too hard
| A
My stones won't take
| E
I get up in the mornin'
| B7
But it's too early to wake
| E
First it's hello, goodbye
| A
Then push and then crash
| E
But we're all gonna make it
| B7   E |
At that million dollar bash
C#m | A   E |
Ooh, baby, ooh-ee
C#m | A   E
Ooh, baby, ooh-ee
| E/B   B7 | E ||
It's that million dollar bash

5. E
Well, I looked at my watch
| A |
I looked at my wrist
E |
Punched myself in the face
B7
With my fist
| E |
I took my potatoes
A |
Down to be mashed
E
Then I made it over
| B7   E |
To that million dollar bash
C#m | A   E |
Ooh, baby, ooh-ee
C#m | A   E
Ooh, baby, ooh-ee
| E/B   B7 | E ||
It's that million dollar bash

Goin' to Acapulco

WORDS AND MUSIC BY
BOB DYLAN

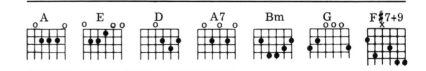

Slowly, with a beat

1. I'm go-ing down_ to Rose Ma-rie's_ She nev-er does me wrong,_

She puts it to_ me

plain as day_ And gives it to me for a song.

It's a wick-ed life ___ but what the hell ___ Oh, ev-
ry-bod-y's got to keep it neat ___ And I'm just the same as the
Taj Ma - hal ___ When it comes to stand-ing on ___ my meat. ___
Goin' to A - ca - pul - co Go - in' on the

run Goin' down ___ to see some girl

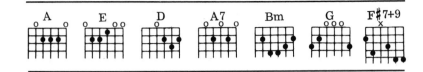

2.

A |E
Now whenever I get up
|D |A | |
And can't find what I need

      |E
I just make it down to Rose Marie's
|D |A | ||
On my white fast faithful steed

A |A7
It's not a bad way to get there
|D |Bm
And I ain't complainin' none
|A |E
If the wheel don't drop and the train don't stop
|D |Bm ||
I'm bound to meet the sun

A |A D |
Goin' to Acapulco
A |G |
Goin' on the run
A |A   D |
Goin' down to see some girl
A |Bm |
Goin' to have some fun
F#7+9 | |
Yeah
A | ||
Goin' to have some fun

3.

A |E |
Now if someone offers me a joke
D |A | |
I just say no thanks

      |E
I try to tell it like it is
|D |A | ||
And keep away from pranks

A | A7 |
Well sometime you know when the well breaks down
D |Bm |
I just go pump on it some
A |E
Rose Marie, she likes to go to big places
|D |Bm ||
And just set there waitin' for me to come

A |A D |
Goin' to Acapulco
A |G |
Goin' on the run
A |A   D |
Goin' down to see some girl
A |Bm |
Goin' to have some fun
F#7+9 | |
Yeah
A | ||
Goin' to have some fun

Apple Suckling Tree

WORDS AND MUSIC BY
BOB DYLAN

Moderately

Old man sail - in' in a din - ghy boat __ Down there, __

Old man down __ is bait - in' a hook On there __

Gon - na pull man down __ on a suck - ling hook __ Gon - na

APPLE SUCKLING TREE

pull man down___ on a suck-ling hook___ Oh yeah!

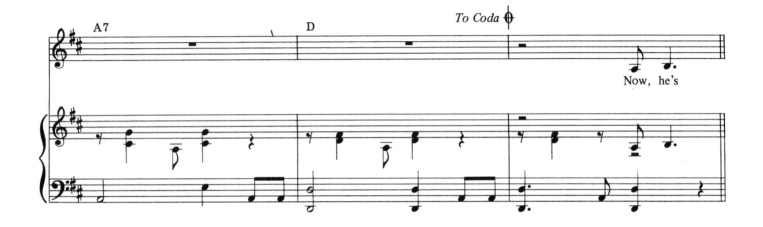

Now, he's

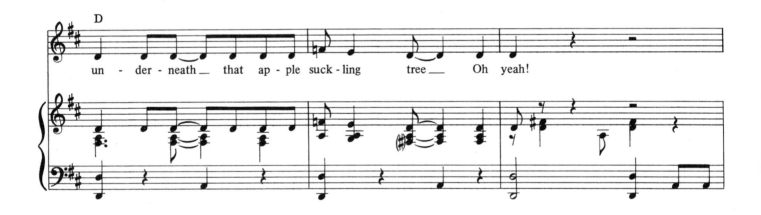

un - der - neath___ that ap - ple suck-ling tree___ Oh yeah!

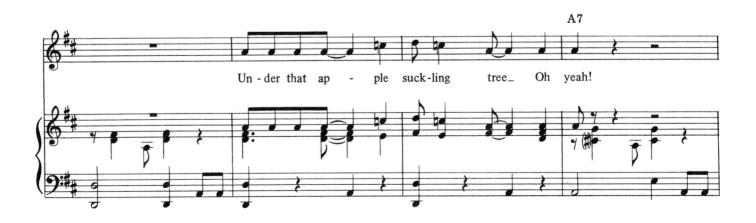

Un - der that ap - ple suck-ling tree___ Oh yeah!

D
I push him back and I stand in line
Oh yeah!
Then I hush my Sadie and stand in line
A7
Oh yeah!
D   **D7**
Then I hush my Sadie and stand in line
G7
I get on board in two-eyed time
D   **A7**   **D**   **‖**
Oh yeah!

D
Under that apple suckling tree
Oh yeah!
Under that apple suckling tree
A7
Oh yeah!
D N.C.   **D7 N.C.**
Underneath that tree
   G N.C.   **G**
There's just gonna be you and me
N.C. D   **A7**
Underneath that apple suckling tree
D   **‖**
Oh yeah!

D
Now, who's on the table, who's to tell me?
Oh yeah!
Who's on the table, who's to tell me?
A7
Oh yeah!
D   **D7**
Who should I tell, oh, who should I tell?
G7
The forty-nine of you go burn in hell
D   **A7**   **D**   **D A D ‖**
Oh underneath that old apple suckling tree

Lo and Behold!

WORDS AND MUSIC BY
BOB DYLAN

(Sung:) Lo and be - hold! Lo and be - hold! Look-in' for __ my

lo and be - hold, Get me out - a here, my dear man! __

2.

D9
I come into Pittsburgh
G9
At six-thirty flat.
|D9
I found myself a vacant seat
|G9
An' I put down my hat.
D9
"What's the matter, Molly, dear,
G9
What's the matter with your mound?"
D9
"What's it to ya, Moby Dick?
G9
This is chicken town!"
D9
Lo and behold! Lo and behold!
G9
Lookin' for my lo and behold,
F   N.C. |N.C.
Get me outa here, my dear man!

3.

D9
I bought my girl
A herd of moose,
G9
One she could call her own.
D9
Well, she came out the very next day
|G9
To see where they had flown.
D9
I'm goin' down to Tennessee,
G9
Get me a truck 'r somethin'.
D9 |G9
Gonna save my money and rip it up!
D9
Lo and behold! Lo and behold!
G9
Lookin' for my lo and behold,
F   N.C. |N.C.
Get me outa here, my dear man!

4.

D9
Now, I come in on a ferris wheel
|G9
An' boys, I sure was slick.
D9
I come in like a ton of bricks,
G9
Laid a few tricks on 'em.
D9
Goin' back to Pittsburgh,
G9
Count up to thirty,
|D9
Round that horn and ride that herd,
|G9
Gonna thread up!
D9
Lo and behold! Lo and behold.
G9
Lookin' for my lo and behold,
F   N.C. |N.C.
Get me outa here, my dear man!

Please, Mrs. Henry

WORDS AND MUSIC BY
BOB DYLAN

Moderately

1. Well, I've al - read - y had two beers I'm read - y for the broom

Please, Mis - sus Hen - ry, won't you Take me to my room? I'm a good ol' boy___ But I've been

sniff - in' too man - y eggs Talk - in' to too man - y peo - ple

Drink - in' too man - y kegs Please, Mis - sus Hen - ry, Mis - sus Hen - ry, please!

Please, Mis-sus Hen-ry, Mis-sus Hen-ry, please! I'm down on my

No Chord

knees _____ An' I ain't got a dime. _____

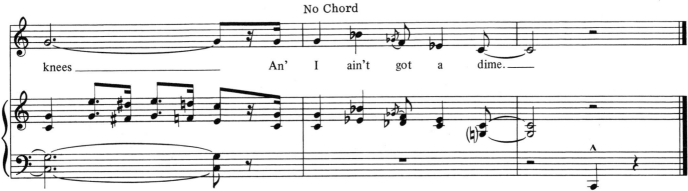

2.

C
Well, I'm groanin' in a hallway
  |F
Pretty soon I'll be mad
C
Please, Missus Henry, won't you
F
Take me to your dad?
  |C
I can drink like a fish
  |G
I can crawl like a snake
  |F
I can bite like a turkey
  |C
I can slam like a drake
              |
Please, Missus Henry, Missus Henry, please!
F
Please, Missus Henry, Missus Henry, please!
  |C
I'm down on my knees
  | N.C. | ||
An' I ain't got a dime

3.

C
Now, don't crowd me, lady
  |F
Or I'll fill up your shoe
  |C
I'm a sweet bourbon daddy
  |F
An' tonight I am blue
  |C
I'm a thousand years old
  |G
And I'm a generous bomb
  |F
I'm T-boned and punctured
C
But I'm known to be calm
              |
Please, Missus Henry, Missus Henry, please!
F
Please, Missus Henry, Missus Henry, please!
  |C
I'm down on my knees
  | N.C. | ||
An' I ain't got a dime

4.

C
Now, I'm startin' to drain
  |F
My stool's gonna squeak
  |C
If I walk too much farther
  |F
My crane's gonna leak
C
Look, Missus Henry
  |G
There's only so much I can do
  |F
Why don't you look my way
  |C
An' pump me a few?
              |
Please, Missus Henry, Missus Henry, please!
F
Please, Missus Henry, Missus Henry, please!
  |C
I'm down on my knees
  | N.C. | ||
An' I ain't got a dime

Tears of Rage

WORDS BY BOB DYLAN
MUSIC BY RICHARD MANUEL

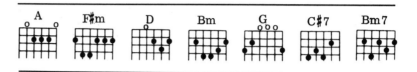

Slowly

With Pedal Throughout

We car-ried you _____ in our arms _____ On
point-ed out _____ the way to go _____ And
all ver-y pain-less _____ When you

In-de-pend-ence Day, And now you'd throw us
scratched your name _____ in sand, Though you just thought _____ it was
went out to _____ re-ceive All that false _____ in-

all a-side _____ And put us on our way. _____ Oh
noth-ing more _____ Than a place for you to stand. _____ Now, I
struc-tion Which we nev-er could be-lieve. _____ And

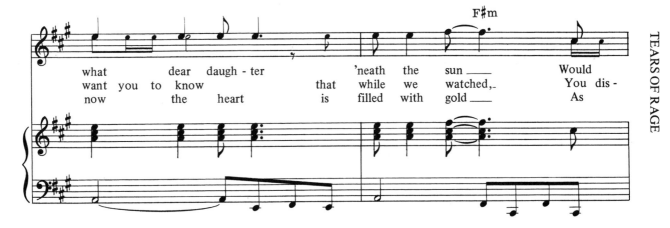

what   dear daugh - ter   'neath the sun ____   Would
want you to know   that while we watched,_   You dis -
now   the heart   is   filled with gold ____   As

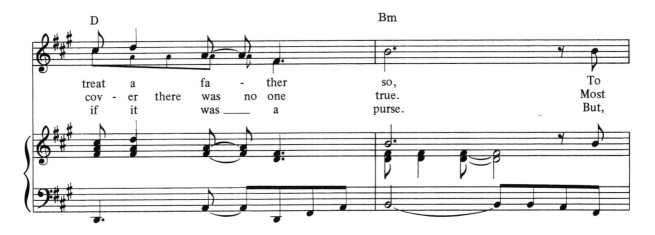

treat a fa - ther   so,   To
cov - er there was no one   true.   Most
if it was ___ a   purse.   But,

wait up - on ___ him hand and foot ___ And
ev - 'ry - bod - y real - ly thought __ It
oh, what kind __ of love is this __ Which

al - ways tell him, "No"? _   Tears of rage,
was a child - ish thing to do. _ Tears of rage,
goes from bad to worse? _ Tears of rage,

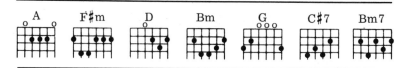

tears of grief, ___ Why must I al-ways be the thief?
tears of grief, ___ Must I al-ways be the thief?
tears of grief, ___ Must I al-ways be the thief?

Come to me now, _ you know We're so a-lone And life is
Come to me now, _ you know We're so ___ low And life is
Come to me now, _ you know We're so ___ low And life is

brief. We
brief. It was brief.

Clothes Line Saga

WORDS AND MUSIC BY
BOB DYLAN

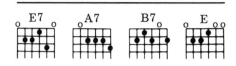

Moderately slow

1. Af-ter a while we took in the clothes, No-bod-y said __ ver-y

much. Just some old wild shirts and a cou-ple pairs of pants Which

no-bod-y real-ly want-ed to touch. Ma-ma come in __ and __

picked up a book __ An' Pa - pa asked her what it was. __

Some - one else __ asked, "What do you care?" Pa - pa said, __ "Well, __ just be -

cause." Then they start - ed __ to take __ back their clothes,

Hang 'em on __ the line. __ It was Jan - u - ar - y the thir - ti - eth

And ev-'ry-bod-y was_ feel-in' fine.

2. E7
The next day everybody got up

Seein' if the clothes were dry.

The dogs were barking, a neighbor passed,

Mama, of course, she said, "Hi!"

A7
"Have you heard the news?" he said, with a grin,

"The Vice-President's gone mad!"

E7
"Where?" "Downtown." "When?" "Last night."

"Hmm, say, that's too bad!"

B7
"Well, there's nothin' we can do about it," said the neighbor,

"It's just somethin' we're gonna have to forget."

E7
"Yes, I guess so," said Ma,

Then she asked me if the clothes was still wet.

3. E7
I reached up, touched my shirt,

And the neighbor said, "Are those clothes yours?"

I said, "Some of 'em, not all of 'em."

He said, "Ya always help out around here with the chores?"

A7
I said, "Sometime, not all the time."

Then my neighbor, he blew his nose

E7
Just as Papa yelled outside.

B7
"Mama wants you t' come back in the house and bring them clothes."

Well, I just do what I'm told,

So, I did it, of course.

E7
I went back in the house and Mama met me

E7 E
And then I shut all the doors.

Yea! Heavy and a Bottle of Bread

WORDS AND MUSIC BY
BOB DYLAN

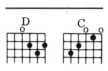

Slowly, with a beat

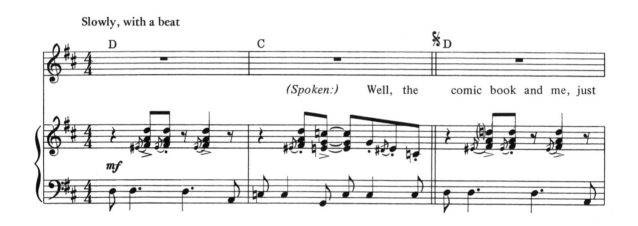

(Spoken:) Well, the comic book and me, just

us, we caught the bus. The poor little chauffeur, though, she was back in bed On the

very next day, with a nose full of pus. (Sung:) Yea! Heav-y and a

Get the loot, don't be slow, we're gon - na catch a trout

Get the loot, don't be slow, we're gon - na catch a trout *(Spoken:)* Now,

pull that drummer out from behind that bottle. Bring me my pipe, we're gonna shake it.

Slap that drummer with a pie that smells.

(Sung:) Take me down to Cal - i - for - nia, ba - by

Take me down to Cal - i - for - nia, ba - by

Take me down to Cal - i - for - nia, ba - by (Spoken:) Yes, the

D. S. al Coda

Coda

Yea! Heav - y and a bot - tle___ of bread.

Tiny Montgomery

WORDS AND MUSIC BY

BOB DYLAN

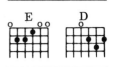

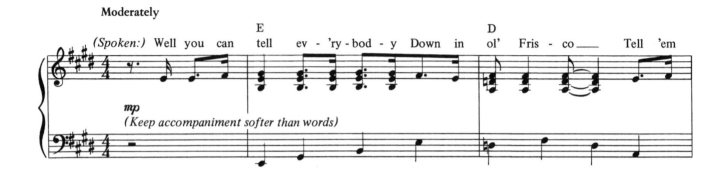

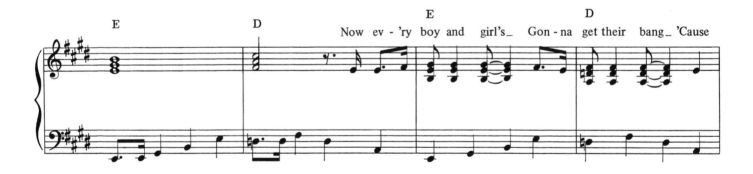

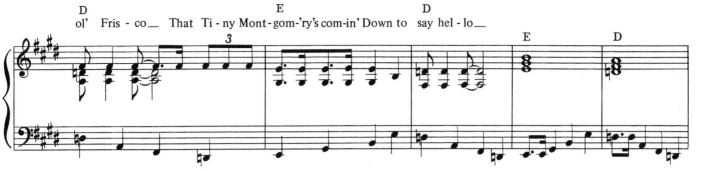

ol' Fris - co__ That Ti - ny Mont-gom-'ry's com-in' Down to say hel - lo__

(Repeat as accompaniment to spoken words and fade)

E
Skinny Moo and
D
Half-track Frank
 |E
They're gonna both be gettin'
D
Outa the tank
E
One bird book
 |D
And a buzzard and a crow
 |E
Tell 'em all
 |D |E |D |E |D ||
That Tiny's gonna say hello

E
Scratch your dad
D
Do that bird
E
Suck that pig
 |D
And bring it on home
E
Pick that drip
 |D
And bake that dough
 |E
Tell 'em all
 |D |E |D |E |D ||
That Tiny says hello

E
Now he's king of the drunks
 |D
An' he squeezes, too
E
Watch out, Lester
D
Take it, Lou
E
Join the monks
D
The C.I.O.
 |E
Tell 'em all
 |D |E |D |E |D ||
That Tiny Montgomery says hello

E
Now grease that pig
 |D
And sing praise
E
Go on out
 |D
And gas that dog
E
Trick on in
D
Honk that stink
E
Take it on down
 |D
And watch it grow
E
Play it low
 |D
And pick it up
E
Take it on in
 |D
In a plucking cup
E
Three-legged man
 |D
And a hot-lipped hoe
E
Tell 'em all
 |D |E |D |E |D ||
Montgomery says hello

E
Well you can tell ev'rybody
 |D
Down in ol' Frisco
 E
Tell 'em all
 |D |E |D |E |D ||
Montgomery says hello

Crash on the Levee
(Down in the Flood)

WORDS AND MUSIC BY
BOB DYLAN

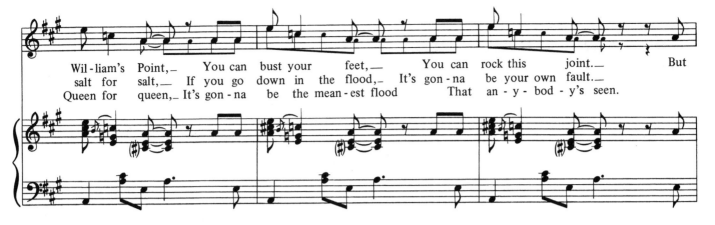

Wil-liam's Point,— You can bust your feet,— You can rock this joint.— But
salt for salt,— If you go down in the flood,— It's gon-na be your own fault.—
Queen for queen,— It's gon-na be the mean-est flood That an-y-bod-y's seen.

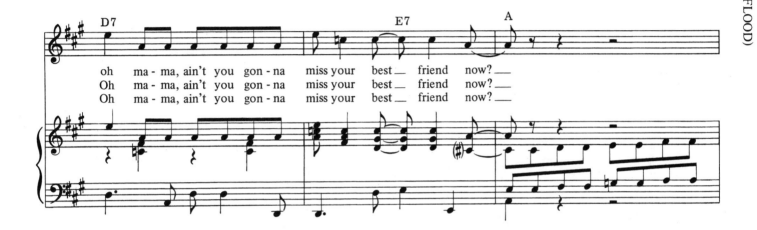

oh ma-ma, ain't you gon-na miss your best — friend now?—
Oh ma-ma, ain't you gon-na miss your best — friend now?—
Oh ma-ma, ain't you gon-na miss your best — friend now?—

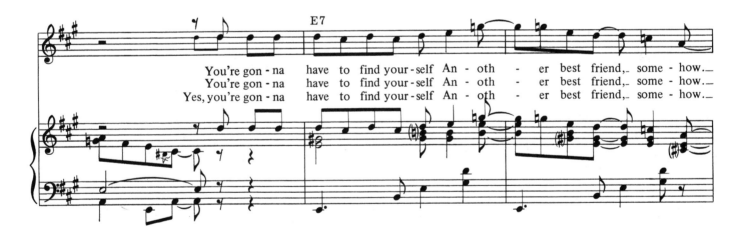

You're gon-na have to find your-self An-oth-er best friend, some-how.—
You're gon-na have to find your-self An-oth-er best friend, some-how.—
Yes, you're gon-na have to find your-self An-oth-er best friend, some-how.—

Now, don't you
Well, that —

You Ain't Goin' Nowhere

WORDS AND MUSIC BY
BOB DYLAN

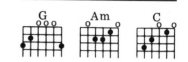

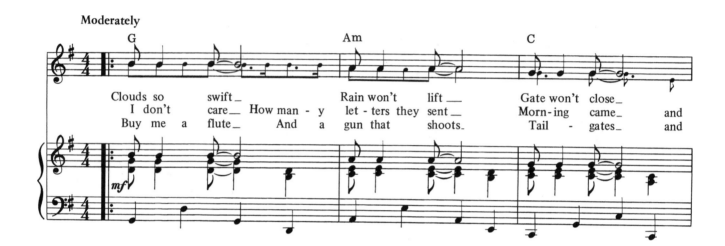

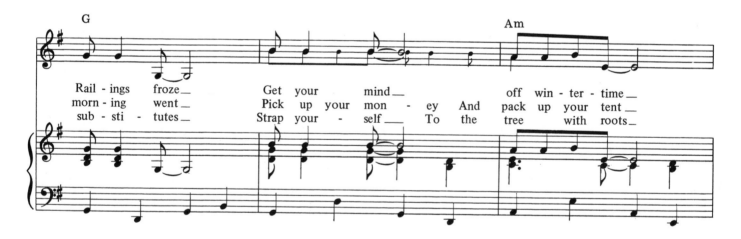

mor-row's the day   My bride's gon - na come   Oh, oh,— are we gon - na fly

Down in the eas - y chair!—   —   Gen-ghis Khan— He

could not keep—   All his kings— Sup - plied with sleep—   We'll climb that hill — no

mat-ter how steep_   When we get up to it.—

Too Much of Nothing

WORDS AND MUSIC BY
BOB DYLAN

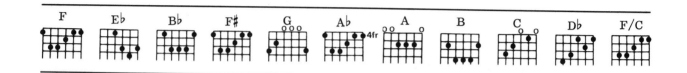

Moderately slow

Now, too much of noth - ing Can make a man feel ill at ease.
Too much of noth - ing Can make a man a - buse a king.
Too much of noth - ing Can turn a man in - to a liar.

One man's tem - per might rise ___ While an - oth - er man's tem-per might freeze.
He can walk the streets and boast like most But he would - n't know a thing.
It can cause one man to sleep on nails And an - oth - er man to eat fire.

In the day of con-fes-sion __ We can-not mock a soul. __ Oh, when
Now, it's all been done be-fore, It's all been writ-ten in the book, __ But when
Ev-'ry - bod - y's do - in' some-thin', __ I heard it in a dream, __ But when

gradual cresc.

there's too much of noth - ing, No one has con - trol.
there's too much of noth - ing, No - bod - y should look.
there's too much of noth - ing, It just makes a fel - la mean.

f

Say hel - lo to Val - e - rie __ Say hel - lo to Viv - i - an __

Send them all my sal - a - ry __ On the wa - ters of ob - liv - i - on.
liv - i - on.

This Wheel's on Fire

WORDS BY BOB DYLAN
MUSIC BY RICK DANKO

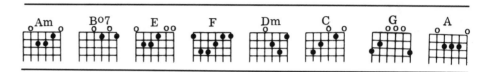

Slowly

If your mem - 'ry serves you well, We were goin' to
mem - 'ry serves you well, I was goin' to
mem - 'ry serves you well, You'll re -

meet ___ a - gain and ___ wait, ___ So I'm goin' to un - pack all ___
con - fis - cate your ___ lace, ___ And wrap ___ it up in ___ a
mem - ber you're the ___ one ___ That called ___ on me to ___ call ___

___ my things And sit be - fore it gets too late. No
sail - or's knot And hide it in your case. If I
___ on them To get you your fa - vors done. And

man ____ a - live ____ will come to you   With an - oth - er ____ tale ___ to tell,
knew ____ for sure ____ that it was yours . . .   But it was oh so ____ hard ___ to tell.
af - ter ev - 'ry plan had failed   And there was noth-ing ____ more_ to tell,

But you know ___ that we ___ shall meet a - gain, ___   If your
But you knew ___ that we ___ would meet a - gain, ___   If your
You knew ___ that we ___ would meet a - gain, ___   If your

mem-'ry ____ serves you well.   This wheel's on
mem-'ry ____ serves you well.   This wheel's on
mem-'ry ____ served you well.   This wheel's on

fire,   Roll - ing down the road, ____
fire,   Roll - ing down the road, ____
fire,   Roll - ing down the road, ____

Am   B°7   E   F   Dm   C   G   A

C   G

Best no - ti - fy my
Best no - ti - fy my
Best no - ti - fy my

F   C   F   G

next of kin,   This wheel shall ex -
next of kin,   This wheel shall ex -
next of kin,   This wheel shall ex -

1.2.
A

3.
A

plode! _____
plode! _____

Am
If your
If your

plode! _____

Open the Door, Homer

WORDS AND MUSIC BY
BOB DYLAN

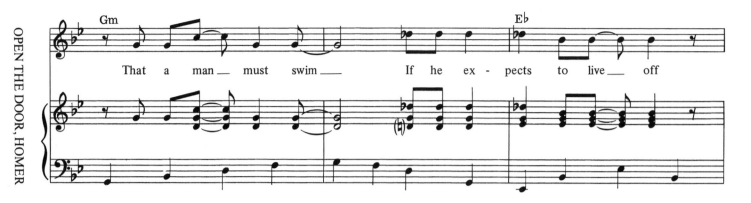

That a man___ must swim___ If he ex - pects to live___ off

Of the fat___ of the land._____ O - pen the

door, Ho - mer, I've heard it said be - fore.___ O - pen the

door, Ho - mer, I've heard it said be - fore ___ But I

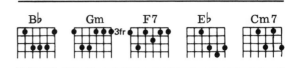

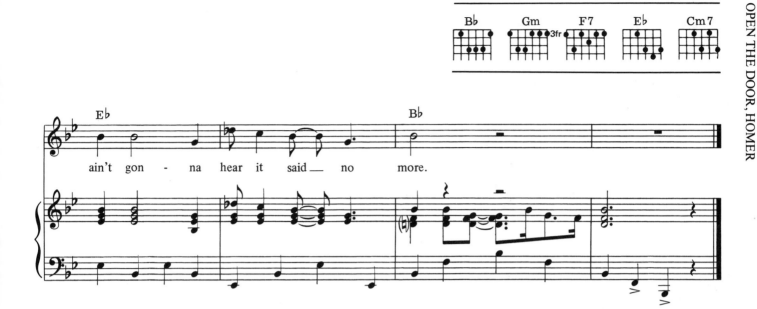

ain't gon - na hear it said — no more.

2. Bb
   Now, there's a certain thing
   | Gm
   That I learned from my friend, Mouse
   Bb | | F7
   A fella who always blushes
   | Bb
   And that is that ev'ryone
   | Gm
   Must always flush out his house
   Eb
   If he don't expect to be
   | F7
   Goin' 'round housing flushes.
   | Cm7 |
   Open the door, Homer,

   I've heard it said before.

   Open the door, Homer,

   I've heard it said before
   | Eb | | Bb | ||
   But I ain't gonna hear it said no more,

3. Bb | | Gm
   "Take care of all your memories"
   | Bb
   Said my friend, Mick
   | F7
   "For you cannot relive them
   | Bb
   And remember when you're out there
   Gm
   Tryin' to heal the sick
   Eb
   That you must always
   | F7
   First forgive them."
   | Cm7 |
   Open the door, Homer,

   I've heard it said before.

   Open the door, Homer,

   I've heard it said before
   | Eb | | Bb | ||
   But I ain't gonna hear it said no more.

Long-Distance Operator

WORDS AND MUSIC BY
BOB DYLAN

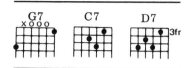

Slow Rock Blues

I got-ta get a mes-sage__ to my ba - by,

You know,_____ she's not just an-y-one.

1.2.3.   4.

2. There are
3. If a
4. Ev - 'ry -

Pedal ✻

2. There are thousands in the phone booth, |G7
  Thousands at the gate. | |
  There are thousands in the phone booth, |C7 |
  Thousands at the gate. |G7
  Ev'rybody wants to make a long-distance call |D7 |
  But you know they're just gonna have to wait. |G7 | ‖

3. If a call comes from Louisiana, G7 | |
  Please, let it ride. |
  If a call comes from Louisiana, |C7 |
  Please, let it ride. |G7
  This phone booth's on fire, |D7 |
  It's getting hot inside. |G7 | ‖

4. Ev'rybody wants to be my friend, G7 |
  But nobody wants to get higher. | |
  Ev'rybody wants to be my friend, |C7 |
  But nobody wants to get higher. |G7 | |
  Long-distance operator, D7 |
  I believe I'm stranglin' on this telephone wire. |G7 | | ‖

Quinn the Eskimo (The Mighty Quinn)

WORDS AND MUSIC BY
BOB DYLAN

Moderately slow, with a beat

Ev - 'ry-bod - y's build - ing the big ships and the boats,_ Some are build-ing mon - u-ments,_ Oth - ers, jot-ting down notes,

Ev - 'ry-bod - y's in de - spair,_ Ev - 'ry girl and boy But when

Quinn the Es - ki - mo gets here, Ev - 'ry - bod - y's gon - na jump_ for joy._

Come all ___ with-out, ___ come all ___ with-in, ___ You'll not see noth-ing like the

might - y Quinn. ___

2. I might - y Quinn. ___
3. A

|Bb   Eb |Bb   Eb
2.   I like to do just like the rest, I like my sugar sweet,
     |Bb   Eb
    But guarding fumes and making haste,
     |Bb   Eb |
    It ain't my cup of meat.
    Bb   Eb
    Ev'rybody's 'neath the trees,
     |Bb   Eb
    Feeding pigeons on a limb
      |Bb   F/A
    But when Quinn the Eskimo gets here,
      |Eb   Bb |
    All the pigeons gonna run to him.
    Bb |F   Bb
    Come all without, come all within,
     |Bb   F/A |Eb/G Bb |Bb Eb |Eb Bb ||
    You'll not see nothing like the mighty Quinn.

|Bb   Eb |Bb   Eb
3.   A cat's meow and a cow's moo, I can recite 'em all,
     |Bb   Eb
    Just tell me where it hurts yuh, honey,
     |Bb   Eb |
    And I'll tell you who to call.
    Bb   Eb
    Nobody can get no sleep,
     |Bb   Eb
    There's someone on ev'ryone's toes
      |Bb   F/A
    But when Quinn the Eskimo gets here,
     |Eb   Bb |
    Ev'rybody's gonna wanna doze.
    Bb |F   Bb
    Come all without, come all within,
     |Bb   F/A |Eb/G Bb ||
    You'll not see nothing like the mighty Quinn.

I Wanna Be Your Lover

WORDS AND MUSIC BY

BOB DYLAN

rain - man leaves in the wolf-man's dis - guise.____

I wan - na be your lov - er, baby,__ I wan - na be__ your

man. I wan - na be your lov - er, ba - by, I don't wan - na be

hers, I wan-na be yours. —

2. G
Well, the undertaker in his midnight suit
Says to the masked man, "Ain't you cute!"
Well, the mask man he gets up on the shelf
And he says, "You ain't so bad yourself." | D7 | | | | G | | | | ||

C7
I wanna be your lover, baby, I wanna be your man.
I wanna be your lover, baby,
I don't wanna be hers, I wanna be yours. | G | | | | ||

3. G
Well, jumpin' Judy can't go no higher.
She had bullets in her eyes, and they fire.
Rasputin he's so dignified,
He touched the back of her head an' he died. | D7 | | | | G | | | | ||

C7
I wanna be your lover, baby, I wanna be your man.
I wanna be your lover, baby,
I don't wanna be hers, I wanna be yours. | G | | | | ||

4. G
Well, Phaedra with her looking glass,
Stretchin' out upon the grass.
She gets all messed up and she faints—
That's 'cause she's ɔ obvious and you ain't. | D7 | | | | G | | | | ||

C7
I wanna be your lover, baby, I wanna be your man.
I wanna be your lover, baby,
I don't wanna be hers, I wanna be yours. | G | | | | ||

Silent Weekend

WORDS AND MUSIC BY
BOB DYLAN

Moderate Blues

Si - lent week - end, _____ My ba - by she gave _ it to me. _
Si - lent week - end, _____ My ba - by she took me by sur -

_ prise. Si - lent week-end, _____ My ba - by she gave _ it to me. _
prise. Si - lent week-end, _____ My ba - by she took _ me by sur -

_ She's act - in' tough and har - dy But I'm sleep - in' at the par - ty, And she's
prise. She's learn - in' a - bout dis - pos - in' But I know I know she's a - doz - in', An' she's

1. leav - in' me in _ mis - er - y. _

2. look - in' at them _ oth - er guys. _

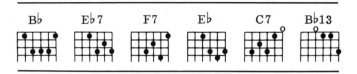

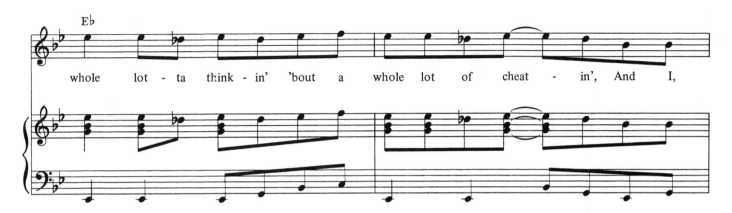

whole lot - ta think - in' 'bout a whole lot of cheat - in', And I,

may-be I did some just to please.__ But I just wal-loped a lot - ta piz - za af - ter

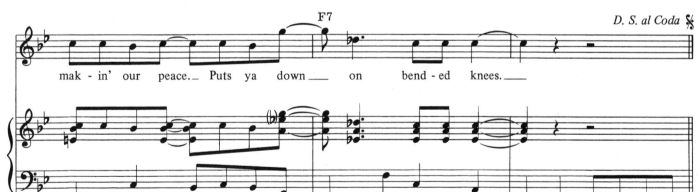

mak - in' our peace.__ Puts ya down__ on bend - ed knees.__

D. S. al Coda 𝄋

o - pen up a pas - sen - ger train.__

Tell Me, Momma

WORDS AND MUSIC BY
BOB DYLAN

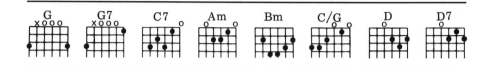

1. Ol' black Bas - com, ___ don't break no mirrors

Cold black wa - ter dog, ___ make no tears ___

You say you love me with what may be love ___

Don't you re - mem - ber mak - in' ba - by love? ___

___ Got your steam drill built ___ and you're

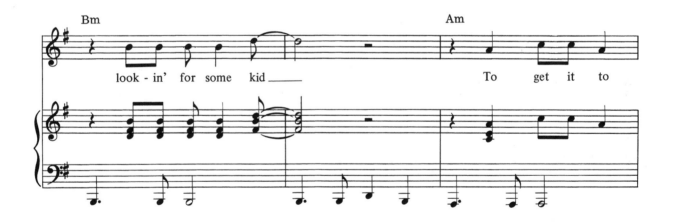

look - in' for some kid ___ To get it to

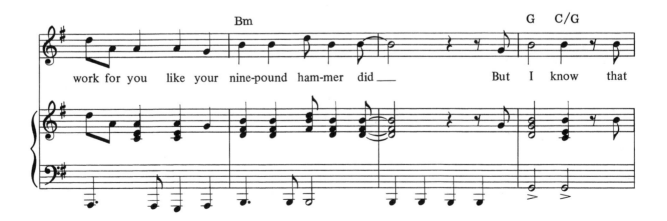

work for you like your nine-pound ham-mer did ___ But I know that

2.

G | | | |
Hey, John, come and get me some candy goods
    | | |G7 |
Shucks, it sure feels like it's in the woods
C7 | | | |
Spend some time on your January trips
G | | |
You got tombstone moose up and your brave-yard whips
  |Am | |Bm
If you're anxious to find out when your friendship's gonna end
Am | |Bm
Come on, baby, I'm your friend!
 |G C/G |G C/G |G C/G |G |
And I know that you know that I know that you show
Am | |Bm | |D | |D7 | ||
Something is tearing up your mind.

G | | | |
Tell me, momma,
  | | | |
Tell me, momma,
  | |Am |
Tell me, momma, what is it?
 |Bm | |G | | | | ||
What's wrong with you this time?

3.

G | | | | |
Ohh, we bone the editor, can't get read
    | | |G7 |
But his painted sled, instead it's a bed
C7 | | | |
Yes, I see you on your window ledge
G | | |
But I can't tell just how far away you are from the edge
  |Am | |Bm |
And, anyway, you're just gonna make people jump and roar
  |Am | |Bm
Whatcha wanna go and do that for?
 |G C/G |G C/G |G C/G |G |
For I know that you know that I know that you know
Am | |Bm | |D | |D7 | ||
Something is tearing up your mind.

G | | | |
Ah, tell me, momma,
  | | | |
Tell me, momma,
  | |Am |
Tell me, momma, what is it?
 |Bm | |G | | | | ||
What's wrong with you this time?

Nothing Was Delivered

WORDS AND MUSIC BY
BOB DYLAN

Moderately slow

1. Nothing was de- livered And I tell this truth to you, Not out of spite or an-ger But sim-ply be-cause it's true. Now, I hope you won't ob-ject to

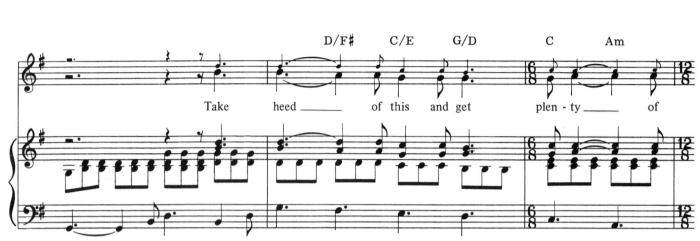

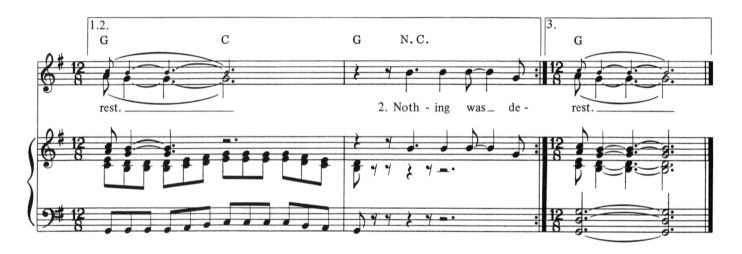

2.
```
N.C.           || C    Am C Am | C
   Nothing was delivered
      Am    C Am   | G    |
   But I can't say I sympathize
                   | D       |
   With what your fate is going to be,
   D       D 7   | G    C | G N.C.
   Yes, for telling all those lies.
                     | C        Am C Am | C
   Now you must provide some answers
      Am    C    Am      | G      |
   For what you sell has not been received,
                      | D         | D
   And the sooner you come up with them,
           D 7   | G    C | G
   The sooner you can leave.


   N.C.     || Em  |          | G      |
   Nothing is better, nothing is best,
       | G    D/F♯ C/E      G/D | 6/8 C Am | 12/8 G
   Take  heed  of  this and get plenty rest.
```

3.
```
N.C.
   (Now you know)
                     || C    Am C Am | C Am
   Nothing was delivered
           C    Am  | G    |
   And it's up to you to say
                  | D      |
   Just what you had in mind
   D         D 7   | G    C | G N.C.
   When you made ev'rybody pay.
                  | C        Am C Am | C
   No, nothing was delivered,
   Am    C    Am      | G    |
   Yes, 'n' someone must explain
                           | D
   That as long as it takes to do this
      | D            D 7  | G    C | G
   Then that's how long that you'll remain.


   N.C.     || Em  |          | G      |
   Nothing is better, nothing is best,
       | G    D/F♯ C/E      G/D | 6/8 C Am | 12/8 G ||
   Take  heed  of  this and get plenty rest.
```

She's Your Lover Now

WORDS AND MUSIC BY
BOB DYLAN

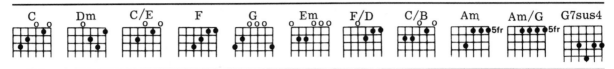

The pawn-bro-ker roared __ Al - so, so, so did the land - lord The scene was so cra - zy, was - n't it? ____ Both were so glad __ To watch me de - stroy __ what I had __

can't you tell?

Some-bod-y had bet-ter ex - plain   She's got her

i - ron chain___   I'd do it, but I, I just can't re-mem-ber how___

You   talk to her___

She's your lov - er now.___

C	Dm	C/E	F	G	Em	F/D	C/B	Am	Am/G	G7sus4

```
                  C          |Dm
       2.    I already assumed
                     |C/E         |F
             That we're in the felony room
                 |C/E         Dm      |C/E    F |G            |
             But I ain't a judge, you don't have to be nice to me
                 |C         |Dm
             But please tell that
                   |C/E             |F
             To your friend in the cowboy hat
                   |C/E     Dm  |C/E  F  |G         |   |
             You know he keeps on sayin' ev'rythin' twice to me
             Em            |
             You know I was straight with you
              |Dm                  |                    |
             You know I've never tried to change you in any way
             Em           |
             You know if you didn't want to be with me
                          |   Dm        |F     |   |G   |   |   |  |
             That you could . . . didn't have to stay.
             G    F  |C/E     F/D      |C       C/B |Am   Am/G  | G7 sus 4   |  |G   |
             Now you stand here sayin' you forgive and forget. Honey, what can I say?
                |Am              |                  |G   |
             Yes, you, you just sit around and ask for ashtrays, can't you reach?
             |Am              |              |G      |  |G   F |C/E   F/D
             I see you kiss her on the cheek ev'rytime she gives a speech
                      |C      Dm       |C/E             Dm
             With her picture books of the pyramid
                  |C    Dm  |C/E     Dm       |
             And her postcards of Billy the Kid
             C    Dm |C/E  F  |G           |   |
             (Why must everybody bow?)
             Am           |G             |
             You better talk to her 'bout it
             F            |C    |G     ||
             You're her lover now.


                  C               |Dm
       3.    Oh, ev'rybody that cares
               |C/E            |F           |
             Is goin' up the castle stairs
             C/E      Dm |C/E       F    |G         |   |
             But I'm not up in your castle, honey
             C              |Dm     |
             It's true, I just can't recall
             C/E           |F
             San Francisco at all
             |C/E  Dm |C/E         F |G         |          |
             I can't even remember El Paso, uh, honey
             Em               |         |
             You never had to be faithful
             Dm                 |        |
             I didn't want you to grieve
             Em                   |
             Oh, why was it so hard for you
                            |Dm          |F      |  |G  |   |   |  |
             If you didn't want to be with me, just to leave?
             G    F  |C/E   F/D         |C       C/B |Am  Am/G  |G7 sus 4 |     |G   |
             Now you stand here while your finger's goin' up my sleeve
                |Am              |  |G   |          |Am  |      |G |   |G F |C/E
             An' you, just what do you do anyway? Ain't there nothin' you can say?
             F/D      |C      Dm    |C/E Dm
             She'll be standin' on the bar soon
                     |C   Dm      |C/E    DM
             With a fish head an' a harpoon
                   |C    Dm |C/E      F    |G       |  |
             An' a fake beard plastered on her brow
             Am               |G          |
             You'd better do somethin' quick
             F              |C    |  ||
             She's your lover now.
```

Don't Ya Tell Henry

WORDS AND MUSIC BY
BOB DYLAN

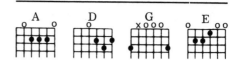

Moderate Rock

1. I went down to the riv - er on a Sat - ur - day morn,__ A -

look - in' a - round __ just to see who's born.__ I

found a lit - tle chick - en down on his knees,__ I

went up and yelled ___ to him, "Please, please, please!" He said, "Don't ___

___ ya tell Hen - ry,   Don't ___

___ ya tell Hen - ry,   Don't ___

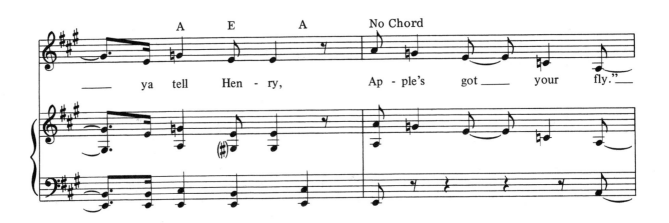

___ ya tell Hen - ry, Ap - ple's got ___ your fly."

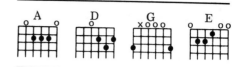

2. A
I went down to the corner at a-half past ten,

I's lookin' around, I wouldn't say when.

I looked down low, I looked above,

And who did I see but the one I love.

| A   D   A   D A |A D A D|
She said, "Don't ya tell Henry,

D   G   D   G D |D G D E|
Don't ya tell Henry,

E   A E   A |
Don't ya tell Henry,

N.C. | | N.C. A ||
Apple's got your fly."

3. A
Now, I went down to the beanery at half past twelve,

A-lookin' around just to see myself.

I spotted a horse and a donkey, too,

I looked for a cow and I saw me a few.

| A   D   A   D A |A D A D |
They said, "Don't ya tell Henry,

D   G   D   G D |D G D E|
Don't ya tell Henry,

E   A   E   A |
Don't ya tell Henry,

N.C. | | N.C. A ||
Apple's got your fly."

4. A
Now, I went down to the pumphouse the other night,

A-lookin' around, it was outa sight.

I looked high and low for that big ol' tree,

I did go upstairs but I didn't see nobody but me.

| A   D   A   D A |A D A D |
I said, "Don't ya tell Henry,

D   G   D   G D |D G D E|
Don't ya tell Henry,

E   A   E   A |
Don't ya tell Henry,

N.C. | | N.C. A ||
Apple's got your fly."

Get Your Rocks Off!

WORDS AND MUSIC BY

BOB DYLAN

Slow Blues

1. You know, there's two ol' maids lay - in' in the bed,

One picked her-self up an' the oth - er one, she said: "Get your rocks off!

Get your rocks off!

(Get 'em off!) Get your rocks

2. Well, you know, there late one night up on Blueberry Hill,

One man turned to the other man and said, with a blood-curdlin' chill, he said:

"Get your rocks off! (Get 'em off!)

Get your rocks off! (Get 'em off!)

Get your rocks off! (Get 'em off!)

Get your rocks off-a me! (Get 'em off!)"

3. Well, you know, we was layin' down around Mink Muscle Creek,

One man said to the other man, he began to speak, he said:

"Get your rocks off! (Get 'em off!)

Get your rocks off! (Get 'em off!)

Get your rocks off! (Get 'em off!)

Get your rocks off-a me! (Get 'em off!)"

4. Well, you know, we was cruisin' down the highway in a Greyhound bus.

All kinds-a children in the side road, they was hollerin' at us, sayin':

"Get your rocks off! (Get 'em off!)

Get your rocks off! (Get 'em off!)

Get your rocks off! (Get 'em off!)

Get your rocks off-a me!"

Hurricane

WORDS BY BOB DYLAN AND JACQUES LEVY
MUSIC BY BOB DYLAN

Moderately

1. Pis-tol shots ring out in the bar __ room night __ En-ter Pat-ty Val-en-tine from the

up-per hall __ She sees the bar-tend-er in a pool of blood __

Cries out, "My God, they killed __ them all!" __ Here comes the sto-ry of the

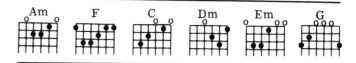

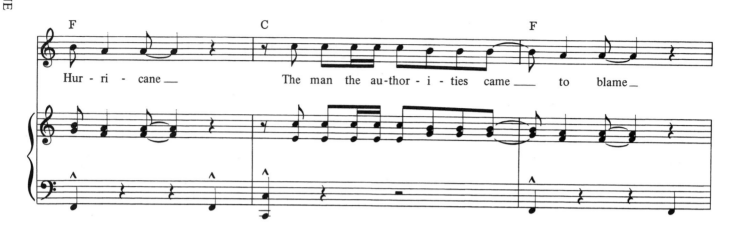

Hur - ri - cane ___ The man the au-thor - i - ties came ___ to blame ___

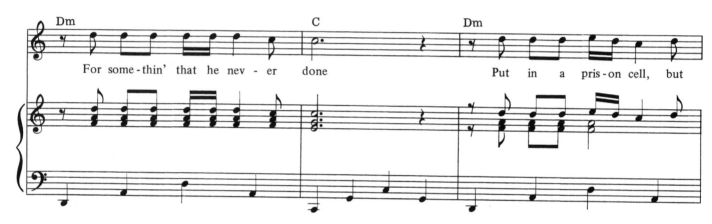

For some-thin' that he nev - er done Put in a pris-on cell, but

one time ___ he could - a been ___ The cham - pi-on of the world.

1. - 10.

11. D. S. (Instrumental) and fade

      Am |F
2. Three bodies lyin' there does Patty see
     |Am |F |
    And another man named Bello, movin' around mysteriously
    Am |F
    "I didn't do it," he says, and he throws up his hands
     |Am |F |C
    "I was only robbin' the register, I hope you understand
                 |F |C
    I saw them leavin'," he says, and he stops
              |F |
    "One of us had better call up the cops"
    Dm |C |
    And so Patty calls the cops
    Dm |C   Em |Am
    And they arrive on the scene with their red lights flashin'
       F |C |G |Am |F |Am |F ||
    In the hot New Jersey night

    Am |F
3. Meanwhile, far away in another part of town
     |Am |F |
    Rubin Carter and a couple of friends are drivin' around
    Am |F
    Number one contender for the middleweight crown
     |Am |F |C
    Had no idea what kinda shit was about to go down
                    |F |C
    When a cop pulled him over to the side of the road
                  |F
    Just like the time before and the time before that
     |Dm |C
    In Paterson that's just the way things go
         |Dm |C   Em |Am
    If you're black you might as well not show up on the street
    F |C |G |Am |F |Am |F
    'Less you wanta draw the heat

     ||Am |F
4. Alfred Bello had a partner and he had a rap for the cops
     |Am |F
    Him and Arthur Dexter Bradley were just out prowlin' around
     |Am |F
    He said, "I saw two men runnin' out, they looked like middleweights
     |Am |F |C
    They jumped into a white car with out-of-state plates"
                  |F |C
    And Miss Patty Valentine just nodded her head
                |F
    Cop said, "Wait a minute boys, this one's not dead"
     |Dm |C |
    So they took him to the infirmary
    Dm |C
    And though this man could hardly see
      Em |Am   F |C |G |Am |F |Am |F ||
    They told him that he could identify the guilty men

    Am |F |
5. Four in the mornin' and they haul Rubin in
    Am |F
    Take him to the hospital and they bring him upstairs
     |Am |F
    The wounded man looks up through his one dyin' eye
     |Am |F |C
    Says, "Wha'd you bring him in here for? He ain't the guy!"
              |F |C
    Yes, here's the story of the Hurricane
                |F |Dm
    The man the authorities came to blame
                  |C |Dm
    For somethin' that he never done
              |C   Em |Am
    Put in a prison cell, but one time he coulda been
      F |C |G |Am |F |Am |F ||
    The champion of the world

    Am |F |
6.   Four months later, the ghettoes are in flame
    Am |F
Rubin's in South America, fightin' for his name
   |Am |F
While Arthur Dexter Bradley's still in the robbery game
   |Am |F |C
And the cops are puttin' the screws to him, lookin' for somebody to blame
               |F |
"Remember that murder that happened in a bar?"
C |F
"Remember you said you saw the getaway car?"
   |Dm |C |
"You think you'd like to play ball with the law?"
Dm |C Em |Am
"Think it mighta been that fighter that you saw runnin' that night?"
     F |C   G |Am |F |Am |F ||
"Don't forget that you are white"

    Am |F |
7.   Arthur Dexter Bradley said, "I'm really not sure"
    Am |F
Cops said, "A poor boy like you could use a break
   |Am |F
We got you for the motel job and we're talkin' to your friend Bello
   |Am |F |C
Now you don't wanta have to go back to jail, be a nice fellow
     |F |C
You'll be doin' society a favor
        |F |Dm
That sonofabitch is brave and gettin' braver
        |C |Dm
We want to put his ass in stir
        |C Em |Am
We want to pin this triple murder on him
    F |C   G |Am |F |Am |F ||
He ain't no Gentleman Jim"

    Am |F
8.   Rubin could take a man out with just one punch
   |Am |F
But he never did like to talk about it all that much
   |Am |F
It's my work, he'd say, and I do it for pay
   |Am |F |C
And when it's over I'd just as soon go on my way
     |F |C
Up to some paradise
               |F |Dm
Where the trout streams flow and the air is nice
        |C |Dm
And ride a horse along a trail
        |C Em
But then they took him to the jail house
   |Am   F |C |G |Am |F |Am |F ||
Where they try to turn a man into a mouse

    Am |F
9.   All of Rubin's cards were marked in advance
   |Am |F
The trial was a pig-circus, he never had a chance
   |Am |F
The judge made Rubin's witnesses drunkards from the slums
   |Am |F |C
To the white folks who watched he was a revolutionary bum
         |F |C
And to the black folks he was just a crazy nigger
        |F
No one doubted that he pulled the trigger
   |Dm |C
And though they could not produce the gun
   |Dm |C Em |Am
The D.A. said he was the one who did the deed
     F |C   G |Am |F |Am |F ||
And the all-white jury agreed

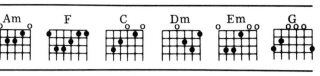

```
    Am              | F
10. Rubin Carter was falsely tried
      | Am              | F                |
    The crime was murder "one", guess who testified?
    Am                | F
    Bello and Bradley and they both baldly lied
        | Am                  | F              | C
    And the newspapers, they all went along for the ride
            | F          | C
    How can the life of such a man
            | F                      | Dm
    Be in the palm of some fool's hand?
                | C          | Dm
    To see him obviously framed
                    | C       Em        | Am
    Couldn't help but make me feel ashamed to live in a land
        F         | C       | G    | Am   | F   | Am   | F
    Where justice is a game
```

```
      || Am                  | F
11.  Now all the criminals in their coats and their ties
        | Am                  | F
    Are free to drink martinis and watch the sun rise
        | Am                  | F
    While Rubin sits like Buddha in a ten-foot cell
      | Am              | F          | C
    An innocent man in a living hell
                | F              | C
    That's the story of the Hurricane
                        | F              |
    But it won't be over till they clear his name
    Dm                      | C      | Dm
    And give him back the time he's done
                  | C    Em          | Am
    Put in a prison cell, but one time he coulda been
        F            | C      | G    |   || D.S. (Instrumental)
    The champion of the world              and fade ƒ.
```

Mozambique

WORDS BY BOB DYLAN AND JACQUES LEVY
MUSIC BY BOB DYLAN

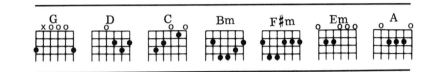

Moderate Reggae beat

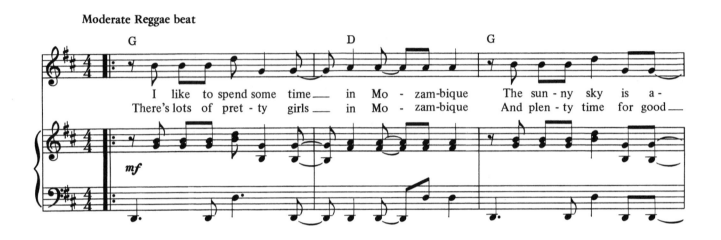

I like to spend some time____ in Mo - zam-bique   The sun - ny sky is a-
There's lots of pret - ty girls ____ in Mo - zam-bique   And plen - ty time for good____

qua - blue   And all the cou - ples danc - ing   cheek___ to cheek
___ ro - mance   And ev - 'ry - bod - y   likes____ to   stop____ and speak

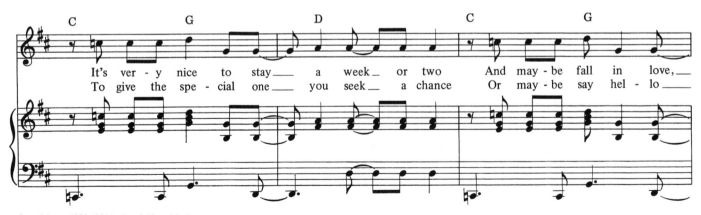

It's ver - y nice to stay____ a week____ or two   And may - be fall in love,____
To give the spe - cial one____ you seek____ a chance   Or may - be say hel - lo____

just me and you. with just a glance. Ly-ing next to her by the o-

cean   Reach-ing out and touch-ing her hand

Whis-per-ing your se-cret e-mo-tion   Mag-ic in a mag-i-cal land.

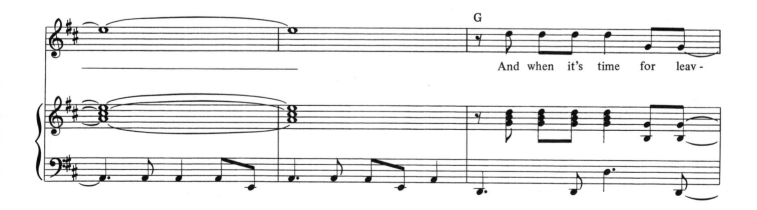

And when it's time for leav-

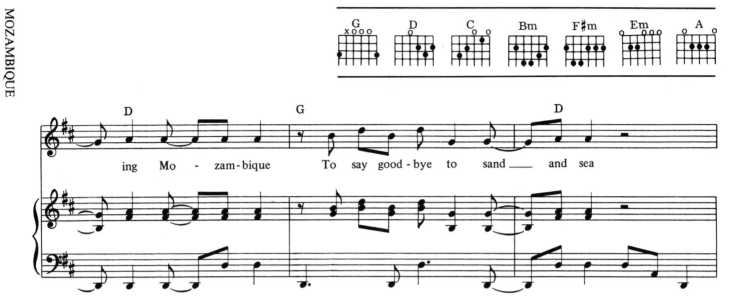

ing Mo - zam-bique To say good-bye to sand ___ and sea

You turn a - round to take ___ a fi - nal peek And you see why it's so ___

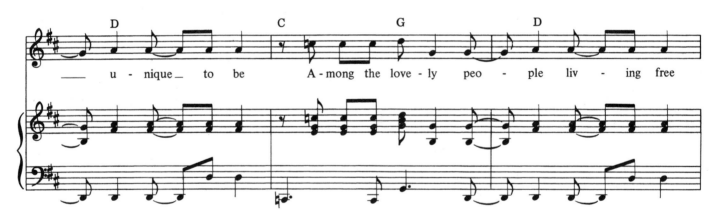

___ u - nique ___ to be A - mong the love - ly peo - ple liv - ing free

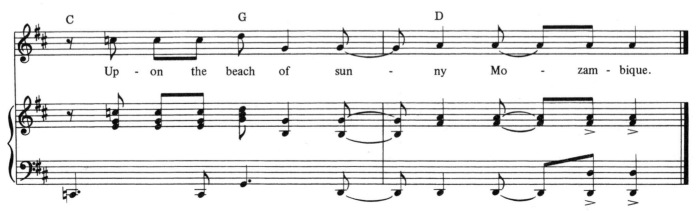

Up - on the beach of sun - ny Mo - zam - bique.

Black Diamond Bay

WORDS BY BOB DYLAN AND JACQUES LEVY
MUSIC BY BOB DYLAN

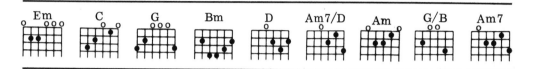

Moderately

1. Up on the white ve-ran - da She wears a neck-tie and a Pa-na-ma hat _

Her pass-port shows a face _ from An-oth-er time and place, she looks

Noth-in' like that _ And all the rem-nants of her

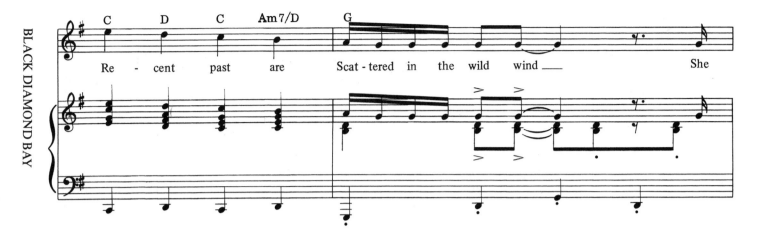

Re - cent past are Scat - tered in the wild wind ___ She

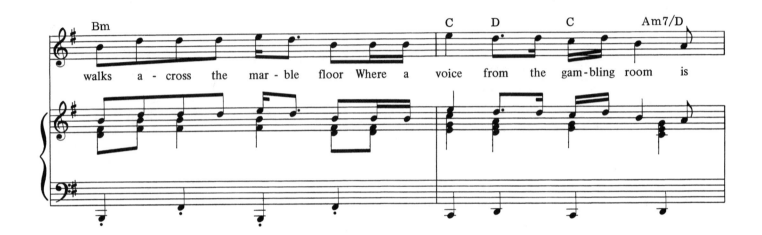

walks a - cross the mar - ble floor Where a voice from the gam - bling room is

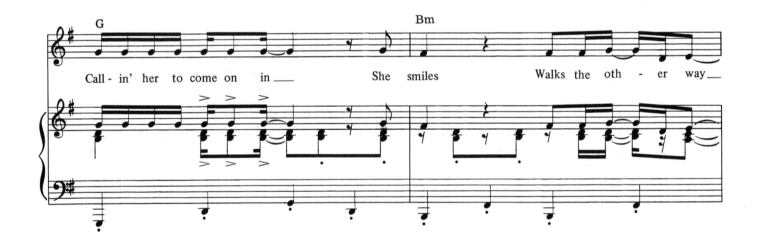

Call - in' her to come on in ___ She smiles Walks the oth - er way ___

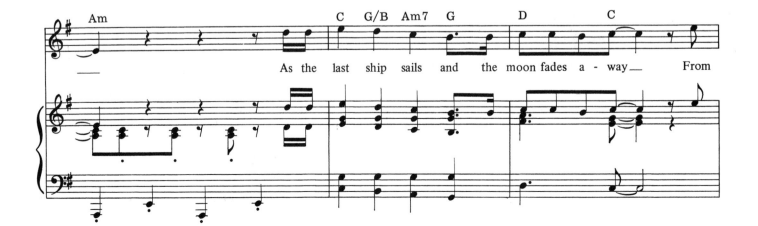

___ As the last ship sails and the moon fades a - way ___ From

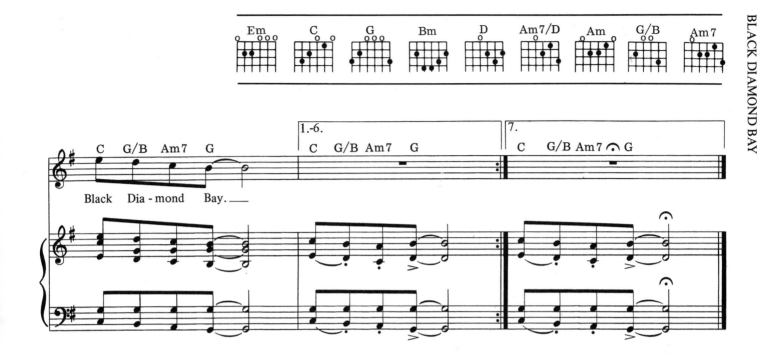

Black Dia - mond Bay.

2. Em
    As the mornin' light breaks open
        |C |
    The Greek comes down and he asks for a rope and a
    G |
    Pen that will write
        |Em |
    "Pardon, Monsieur," the desk clerk says
    C
    Carefully removes his fez
            |G |
    "Am I hearin' you right?"
        |Bm
    And as the yellow fog is liftin'
        |C   D C Am7/D |
    The Greek is quickly
    G
    Headin' for the second floor
        |Bm |
    She passes him on the spiral staircase
    C   D   C   Am7/D |
    Thinkin' he's the
    G
    Soviet Ambassador
        |Bm
    She starts to speak
            |Am
    But he walks away
        |C   G/B   Am7 G |D   C
    As the storm clouds rise and the palm branches sway
        |C   G/B Am7 G |C G/B Am7 G
    On Black Diamond Bay.

3. ‖Em
    A soldier sits beneath the fan
        |C |
    Doin' business with a tiny man who
    G | |
    Sells him a ring
    Em
    Lightning strikes, the lights blow out
        |C
    The desk clerk wakes and begins to shout
            |G |
    "Can you see anything?"
        |Bm
    Then the Greek appears on the second floor
        |C   D   C   Am7/D |
    In his bare feet with a
    G
    Rope around his neck
        |Bm |
    While a loser in the gambling room
    C   D   C   Am7/D |
    Lights up a candle, says
    G
    "Open up another deck"
        |Bm
    But the dealer says
                    |Am
    "Attendez-vous, s'il vous plaît"
        |C   G/B Am7 G |D   C
    As the rain beats down and the cranes fly away
        |C   G/B Am7 G |C G/B Am7 G
    From Black Diamond Bay.

Em   C   G   Bm   D   Am7/D   Am   G/B   Am7

4.
|| Em
The desk clerk heard the woman laugh
| C
As he looked around in the aftermath
| G
And the soldier got tough
| Em
He tried to grab the woman's hand
C
Said, "Here's a ring, it cost a grand." She said
G
"That ain't enough"
| Bm
Then she ran upstairs to pack her bags
| C   D   C   Am7/D |
While a horse-drawn taxi
G
Waited at the curb
| Bm
She passed the door that the Greek had locked
| C   D   C   Am7/D|
Where a hand-written sign read
 G
"Do Not Disturb"
| Bm | Am
She knocked upon it anyway
| C   G/B   Am7 G | D   C
As the sun went down and the music did play
| C   G/B Am7 G | C G/B Am7 G ||
On Black Diamond Bay.

5.
Em
"I've got to talk to someone quick!"
| C |
But the Greek said, "Go away," and he kicked the
G | |
Chair to the floor
Em
He hung there from the chandelier
| C |
She cried, "Help, there's danger near, please
G |
Open up the door!"
| Bm
Then the volcano erupted
| C D C   Am7/D |
And the lava flowed down
G
From the mountain high above
| Bm
The soldier and the tiny man
| C   D   C Am7/D |
Were crouched in the corner
G
Thinking of forbidden love
| Bm
But the desk clerk said
| Am
"It happens every day"
| C   G/B Am7 G | D   C
As the stars fell down and the fields burned away
| C   G/B Am7 G | C G/B   Am7   G ||
On Black Diamond Bay.

6.
Em
As the island slowly sank
| C
The loser finally broke the bank
| G
In the gambling room
| Em
The dealer said

"It's too late now
| C
You can take your money
|
But I don't know how you'll
G |
Spend it in the tomb"
| Bm
The tiny man bit the soldier's ear
| C   D   C Am7/D
As the floor caved in and
| G |
The boiler in the basement blew
Bm
While she's out on the balcony
| C   D   C   Am7/D
Where a stranger tells her
| G
"My darling, je vous aime beaucoup"
| Bm | Am
She sheds a tear and then begins to pray
| C   G/B Am7 G | D   C
As the fire burns on and the smoke drifts away
| C   G/B Am7 G | C   G/B Am7 G
From Black Diamond Bay.

7.
|| Em
I was sittin' home alone one night
| C |
In L.A. watchin' old Cronkite on the
G |
Seven o'clock news
| Em |
It seems there was an earthquake that
C
Left nothin' but a Panama hat
| G |
And a pair of old Greek shoes
| Bm
Didn't seem like much was happenin'
| C   D C Am7/D |
So I turned it off and
G
Went to grab another beer
| Bm
Seems like every time you turn around
| C   D   C   Am7/D |
There's another hard luck
G
Story that you're gonna hear
| Bm
And there's really nothin'
| Am
Anyone can say
| C   G/B Am7 G | D   C
And I never did plan to go anyway
| C   G/B Am7 G | C   G/B Am7 G ||
To Black Diamond Bay.

One More Cup of Coffee
(Valley Below)

WORDS AND MUSIC BY
BOB DYLAN

1. Your breath is sweet ____ Your eyes are like

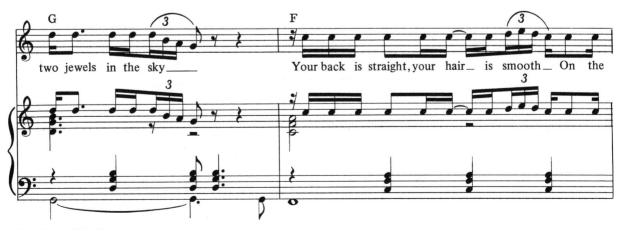

two jewels in the sky ____ Your back is straight, your hair __ is smooth __ On the

pil-low where_ you lie ___ But I don't sense af - fec - tion ___

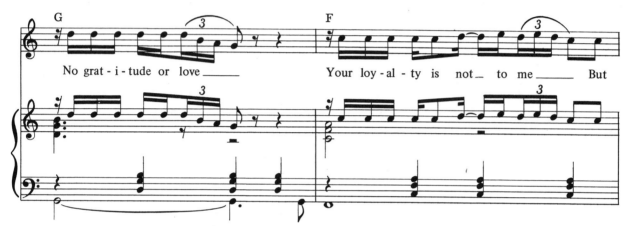

No grat - i - tude or love ___ Your loy - al - ty is not_ to me ___ But

to the stars_ a - bove___ One more cup of cof-fee for the road_

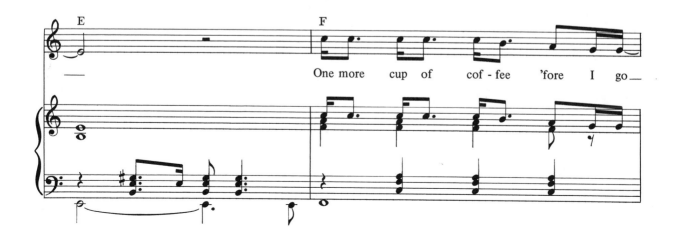

___ One more cup of cof - fee 'fore I go___

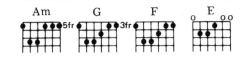

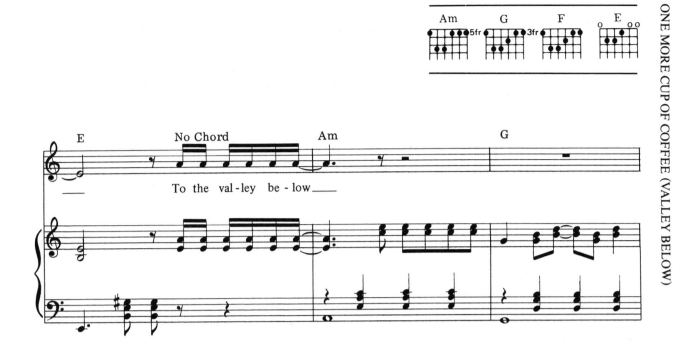

To the val-ley be-low_____

1. 2.

2. Your
3. Your

3.

‖ Am
2.   Your daddy he's an outlaw
        | G |
      And a wanderer by trade
      F
      He'll teach you how to pick and choose
        | E |
      And how to throw the blade
      Am |
      He oversees his kingdom
      G |
      So no stranger does intrude
      F
      His voice it trembles as he calls out for
        | E   ‖
      Another plate of food

      F | E |
      One more cup of coffee for the road
      F | E
      One more cup of coffee 'fore I go
      N.C. | Am | G | F | E
      To the valley below

‖ Am
3.   Your sister sees the future
        | G |
      Like your mama and yourself
      F
      You've never learned to read or write
        | E |
      There's no books upon your shelf
        | Am |
      And your pleasure knows no limits
        | G |
      Your voice is like a meadow lark
        | F |
      But your heart is like an ocean
        | E   ‖
      Mysterious and dark

      F | E |
      One more cup of coffee for the road
      F | E
      One more cup of coffee 'fore I go
      N.C. | Am | G | F | E | Am ‖
      To the valley below

Oh, Sister

WORDS BY BOB DYLAN AND JACQUES LEVY
MUSIC BY BOB DYLAN

Oh, sis - ter, when I come to lie in your arms,
Oh, sis - ter, am I not a broth - er to you

You should not treat me like a stran - ger.
And one de - serv - ing of af - fec - tion?

Our Fa - ther would not like the way that you act,
And is our pur - pose not the same on this earth?

And you must re - al - ize The dan - ger.
To love and fol - low His di - rec - tion.

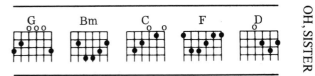

We grew up to-geth-er from the cra-dle to the grave.__ We

died and were re-born and then Mys-te-ri-ous-ly saved.__ Oh, sis-ter, when I come to

knock on your door,__ Don't turn a-way, you'll cre-ate sor-row.__

Time is an o-cean but it ends at the shore.__ You may not see me To-mor-row.

Isis

WORDS BY BOB DYLAN AND JACQUES LEVY
MUSIC BY BOB DYLAN

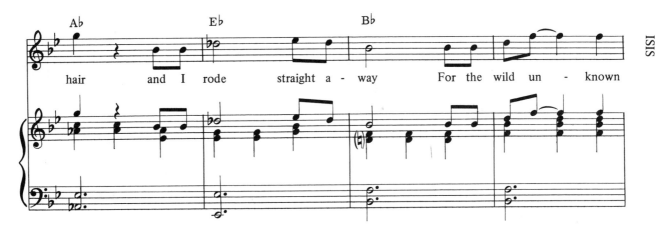

hair and I rode straight a - way For the wild un - known

coun - try___ where I could not___ go wrong.

1.-12.   13.

2. I

||Bb |Ab |Eb |Bb
2. I came to a high place of darkness and light.
   | |Ab |Eb |Bb
   The dividing line ran through the center of town.
   | |Ab |Eb |Bb
   I hitched up my pony to a post on the right,
   | |Ab |Eb |Bb | | | |
   Went into a laundry to wash my clothes down.

||Bb |Ab |Eb |Bb
3. A man in the corner approached me for a match.
   | |Ab |Eb |Bb
   I knew right away he was not ordinary.
   | |Ab |Eb |Bb
   He said, "Are you lookin' for somethin' easy to catch?"
   | |Ab |Eb |Bb | | | |
   I said, "I got no money." He said, "That ain't necessary."

||Bb |Ab |Eb |Bb
4. We set out that night for the cold in the North.
   | |Ab |Eb |Bb
   I gave him my blanket, he gave me his word.
   | |Ab |Eb |Bb
   I said, "Where are we goin'?" He said we'd be back by the fourth.
   | |Ab |Eb |Bb | | | |
   I said, "That's the best news that I've ever heard."

||Bb |Ab |Eb |Bb
5. I was thinkin' about turquoise, I was thinkin' about gold,
   | |Ab |Eb |Bb
   I was thinkin' about diamonds and the world's biggest necklace.
   | |Ab |Eb |Bb
   As we rode through the canyons, through the devilish cold,
   | |Ab |Eb |Bb | | | |
   I was thinkin' about Isis, how she thought I was so reckless.

Bb   Ab   Eb

    ‖ Bb | Ab | Eb | Bb
6. How she told me that one day we would meet up again,
    | | Ab | Eb | Bb
    And things would be different the next time we wed,
    | | Ab | Eb | Bb
    If I only could hang on and just be her friend.
    | | Ab | Eb | Bb | | | |
    I still can't remember all the best things she said.

    ‖ Bb | Ab |Eb | Bb
7. We came to the pyramids all embedded in ice.
    | | Ab | Eb | Bb
    He said, "There's a body I'm tryin' to find,
    | | Ab | Eb | Bb
    If I carry it out it'll bring a good price."
    | | Ab | Eb | Bb | | | |
    'Twas then that I knew what he had on his mind.

    ‖ Bb | Ab | Eb | Bb
8. The wind it was howlin' and the snow was outrageous.
    | | Ab | Eb | Bb
    We chopped through the night and we chopped through the dawn.
    | | Ab | Eb | Bb
    When he died I was hopin' that it wasn't contagious,
    | | Ab | Eb | Bb | | |
    But I made up my mind that I had to go on.

    ‖Bb | Ab | Eb | Bb
9. I broke into the tomb, but the casket was empty.
        | | Ab | Eb | Bb
    There was no jewels, no nothin', I felt I'd been had.
    | | Ab | Eb | Bb
    When I saw that my partner was just bein' friendly,
    | | Ab | Eb | Bb | | |
    When I took up his offer I must-a been mad.

    ‖Bb | Ab | Eb | Bb |
10. I picked up his body and I dragged him inside,
           | Ab | Eb | Bb
    Threw him down in the hole and I put back the cover.
    | | Ab | Eb | Bb
    I said a quick prayer and I felt satisfied.
    | | Ab | Eb |Bb | | | |
    Then I rode back to find Isis just to tell her I love her.

    ‖ Bb | Ab |Eb | Bb |
11. She was there in the meadow where the creek used to rise.
    | Ab | Eb | Bb |
    Blinded by sleep and in need of a bed,
    ' | Ab | Eb | Bb
    I came in from the East with the sun in my eyes.
    | | Ab | Eb | Bb | | | |
    I cursed her one time then I rode on ahead.

    ‖ Bb | Ab | Eb | Bb
12. She said, "Where ya been?" I said, "No place special."
    | | Ab | Eb | Bb
    She said, "You look different." I said, "Well, I guess."
    | | Ab | Eb | Bb
    She said, "You been gone." I said, "That's only natural."
    | | Ab | Eb | Bb | | | | ‖
    She said, "You gonna stay?" I said, "If ya want me to, yes."

    Bb | Ab | Eb | Bb
13. Isis, oh, Isis, you mystical child.
    | | Ab | Eb | Bb
    What drives me to you is what drives me insane.
    | | Ab | Eb | Bb
    I still can remember the way that you smiled
    | | Ab | Eb | Bb | | | | ‖
    On the fifth day of May in the drizzlin' rain.

Golden Loom

WORDS AND MUSIC BY
BOB DYLAN

Moderately

1. Smok-y au-tumn night ____ Stars up __ in the sky ____

I see the sail - in' ____ boats ____

A - cross the bay go by. ____

Eu - ca - lyp - tus trees ____ Hang a - bove the street ____

GOLDEN LOOM

And then I turn my head

For you're ap-proach-in' me.

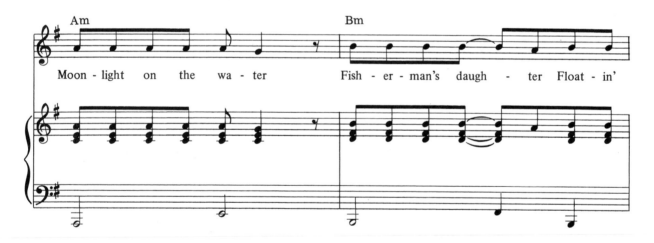

Moon - light on the wa - ter   Fish - er - man's daugh - ter   Float - in'

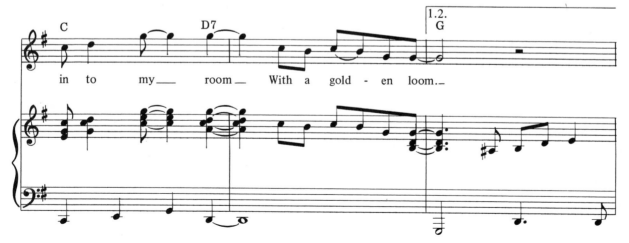

in to my___ room ___ With a gold - en loom. ___

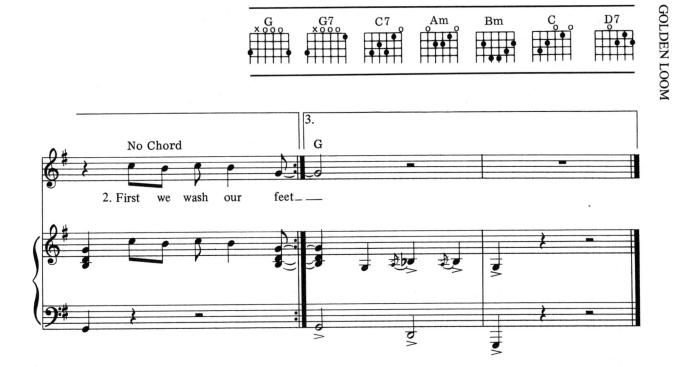

No Chord

2. First we wash our feet —

3.

G

2. N.C.   ‖ G |
    First we wash our feet
                | |
    Near the immortal shrine
                | |
    And then our shadows meet
                | | G 7
    And then we drink the wine
              | C 7 |
    I see the hungry clouds
                | |
    Up above your face
              | G |
    And then the tears roll down
              | |
    What a bitter taste
          | A m
    And then you drift away
        | B m
    On a summer's day
          | C   D 7 | D 7
    Where the wild flowers bloom
                | G | G N.C.
    With your golden loom

3.   ‖ G |
    I walk across the bridge
                    | |
    In the dismal light
                    | |
    Where all the cars are stripped
                    | | G 7
    Between the gates of night
              | C 7 |
    I see the trembling lion
                | |
    With the lotus flower tail
                | G |
    And then I kiss your lips
              | |
    As I lift your veil
            | A m
    But you're gone and then all
        | B m
    I seem to recall
          | C   D 7 | D 7
    Is the smell of perfume
                  | G | ‖
    And your golden loom

Joey

WORDS BY BOB DYLAN AND JACQUES LEVY
MUSIC BY BOB DYLAN

asked him why___ it had to be that way___ Well, he an-swered,"Just be-cause"___

Lar-ry was the old-est   Jo-ey was next___ to last ___

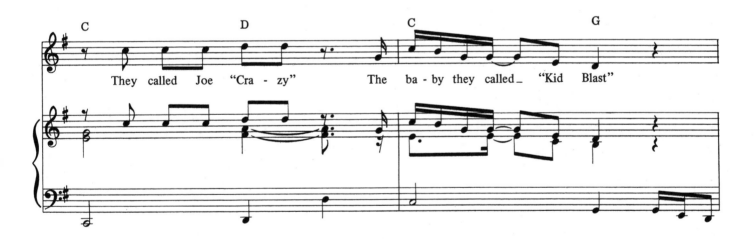

They called Joe "Cra-zy"   The ba-by they called_ "Kid Blast"

Some say they lived off gam-bling   And run-nin' num-bers too   It

JOEY

al - ways seemed_ they got caught be - tween_ The mob and the men in blue_

Jo - ey,___ Jo - ey___ King of the streets,

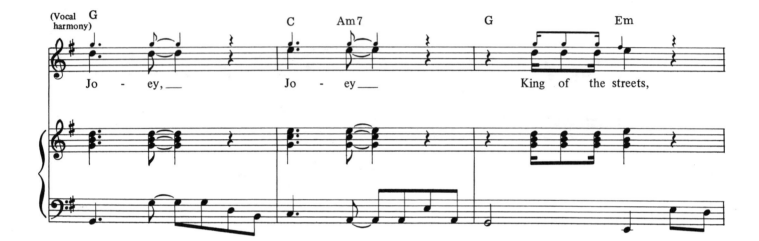

child of clay Jo - ey,___ Jo - ey___

What made them want to come and blow you a - way?___

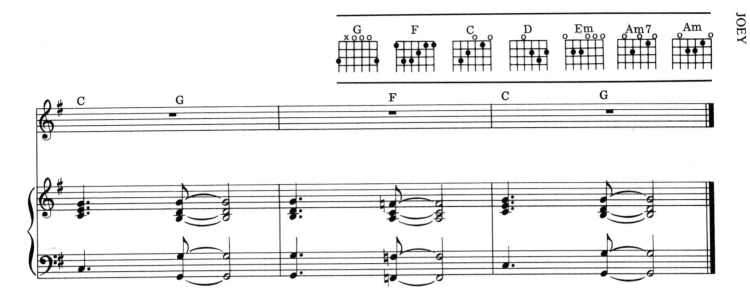

2.
    ‖C   D
  There was talk they killed their rivals
    |C   G |
  But the truth was far from that
  C   D
  No one ever knew for sure
    |C   G
  Where they were really at
     |C   D
  When they tried to strangle Larry
    |C   G
  Joey almost hit the roof
     |Em   G |
  He went out that night to seek revenge
  C   Am
  Thinkin' he was bullet-proof

    ‖C   D
  The war broke out at the break of dawn
   |C   G |
  It emptied out the streets
  C   D
  Joey and his brothers
    |C   G
  Suffered terrible defeats
    |C   D
  Till they ventured out behind the lines
   |C   G
  And took five prisoners
    |Em   G |
  They stashed them away in a basement
  C   Am   ‖
  Called them amateurs

  C   D |
  The hostages were tremblin'
  C   G |
  When they heard a man exclaim
  C   D
  "Let's blow this place to Kingdom Come
     |C   G
  Let Con Edison take the blame"
    |C   D
  But Joey stepped up, he raised his hand
     |C   G
  Said, "We're not those kind of men
   |Em   G
  It's peace and quiet that we need
   |C   Am   ‖
  To go back to work again"

  G |C Am |G
  Joey, Joey
      Em |C Am |
  King of the streets, child of clay
  G |C Am |G
  Joey, Joey
      F |C Am |G F|C G|G F|C G
  What made them want to come and blow you away?

```
        ‖ C              D
3.   The police department hounded him
        | C              G
     They called him Mr. Smith
        | C              D
     They got him on conspiracy
              | C              G    |
     They were never sure who with
       C              D
     "What time is it?" said the judge
       | C              G    |
     To Joey when they met
       Em             G
     "Five to ten," said Joey
                    | C              Am     ‖
     The judge says, "That's exactly what you get"


       C                    D
     He did ten years in Attica
          | C              G      |
     Reading Nietzsche and Wilhelm Reich
       C              D
     They threw him in the hole one time
        | C         G         |
     For tryin' to stop a strike
       C              D
     His closest friends were black men
            | C              G       |
     'Cause they seemed to understand
     Em                 G
     What it's like to be in society
        | C              Am     ‖
     With a shackle on your hand


       C                    D    |
     When they let him out in '71
     C              G         |
     He'd lost a little weight
     C                    D
     But he dressed like Jimmy Cagney
           | C              G    |
     And I swear he did look great
     C              D
     He tried to find the way back in
        | C         G         |
     To the life he left behind
     Em                 G
     To the boss he said, "I have returned
        | C              Am      ‖
     And now I want what's mine"


       G    | C Am    | G
     Joey, Joey
                 Em   | C         Am      |
     King of the streets, child of clay
     G    | C  Am    | G
     Joey, Joey
              F              | C      Am      | G    F | C    G | G    F | C    G
     Why did they have to come and blow you away?


        ‖ G              D
4.   It was true that in his later years
        | C              G    |
     He would not carry a gun
       C              D                    |
     "I'm around too many children," he'd say
       C              G
     "They should never know of one"
        | C              D
     Yet he walked right into the clubhouse
          | C              G |
     Of his life-long deadly foe
     Em             G
     Emptied out the register
        | C              Am           ‖
     Said, "Tell 'em it was Crazy Joe"
```

G   F   C   D   Em   Am7   Am

```
C              D
One day they blew him down
    |C        G        |
In a clam bar in New York
C                   D
He could see it comin' through the door
        |C             G |
As he lifted up his fork
C              D
He pushed the table over
   |C              G
To protect his family
        |Em        G
Then he staggered out into the streets
     |C      Am      ||
Of Little Italy


G   |C Am  |G
Joey, Joey
          Em  |C     Am    |
King of the streets, child of clay
G   |C Am  |G
Joey, Joey
        F              |C     Am    |G  F|C  G|G  F|C  G
What made them want to come and blow you away?
```

5.
```
        ||C              D
   Sister Jacqueline and Carmela
           |C       G      |
   And Mother Mary all did weep
   C              D
   I heard his best friend Frankie say
           |C            G   |
   "He ain't dead, he's just asleep."
   C                      D          |
   Then I saw the old man's limousine
   C                G
   Head back towards the grave
   |Em              G
   I guess he had to say one last goodbye
      |C             Am
   To the son that he could not save
```

```
     ||C                   D
   The sun turned cold over President Street
        |C           G        |
   And the town of Brooklyn mourned
   C                D
   They said a mass in the old church
        |C          G
   Near the house where he was born
     |C             D
   And someday if God's in heaven
      |C           G
   Overlookin' his preserve
   |Em              G
   I know the men that shot him down
     |C             Am      ||
   Will get what they deserve
```

```
G   |C Am  |G
Joey, Joey
          Em  |C     Am    |
King of the streets, child of clay
G   |C Am  |G
Joey, Joey
        F              |C     Am    |G  F|C  G|G  F|C  G  ||
What made them want to come and blow you away?
```

Romance in Durango

WORDS BY BOB DYLAN AND JACQUES LEVY
MUSIC BY BOB DYLAN

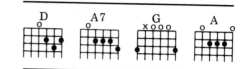

Moderately slow

1. Hot chil-i pep-pers in the blis-ter-ing sun,____

Dust on my face ____ and my cape.____

Me and Mag-da-le-na on ____ the run,____

I think this time we shall es - cape.

Sold my gui - tar to the bak - er's son

For a few crumbs___ and a place to hide.___

But I can get an - oth - er one___ And I'll

play for Mag - da - le - na as we ride.___ No

llo - res, mi que - ri - da, Di - os nos vi - gi - la,___ Soon the horse___ will take us to Du-

ran - go. A - gá - rra - me, mi vi - da, Soon the

des - ert will be gone.___ Soon you will be danc - ing the fan - dan - go.

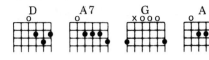

2.
D | A7 |
Past the Aztec ruins and the ghosts of our people.
                | G D | D
Hoofbeats like castanets on stone.
               |$\frac{1}{4}$ |$\frac{4}{4}$ A7
At night I dream of bells in the village steeple,
                         | G D ||
Then I see the bloody face of Ramon.

D | A7 |
Was it me that shot him down in the cantina?
            | G D | D
Was it my hand that held the gun?
         |$\frac{1}{4}$ |$\frac{4}{4}$ A7
Come, let us fly, my Magdalena,
                    | G D |$\frac{1}{4}$ D
The dogs are barking and what's done is done.

       |$\frac{4}{4}$ A |
No llores, mi querida,
                  |
Dios nos vigila,
                     | G D |$\frac{1}{4}$ D
Soon the horse will take us to Durango.
    |$\frac{4}{4}$ A
Agárrame, mi vida,
                   |
Soon the desert will be gone.
              | G D ||
Soon you will be dancing the fandango.

3.
D | A7
At the corrida we'll sit in the shade
                   | G D | D
And watch the young torero stand alone.
                |$\frac{1}{4}$ |$\frac{4}{4}$ A7
We'll drink tequila where our grandfathers stayed
                | G D | D ||
When they rode with Villa into Toreon.

D | A7
Then the padre will recite the prayers of old
               | G D | D
In the little church this side of town.
             |$\frac{1}{4}$ |$\frac{4}{4}$ A7
I will wear new boots and an earring of gold.
                        | G D | D ||
You'll shine with diamonds in your wedding gown.

D | A7 |
The way is long but the end is near.
              | G D | D
Already the fiesta has begun.
           |$\frac{1}{4}$ |$\frac{4}{4}$ A7
The face of God will appear
                     G   D |$\frac{1}{4}$ D
With His serpent eyes of obsidian.

       |$\frac{4}{4}$ A |
No llores, mi querida,
                  |
Dios nos vigila,
                     | G D |$\frac{1}{4}$ D
Soon the horse will take us to Durango.
    |$\frac{4}{4}$ A
Agárrame, mi vida,
                   |
Soon the desert will be gone.
              | G D || D
Soon you will be dancing the fandango.

4.
                 | A7 |
Was that the thunder that I heard?
                      | G D | D
My head is vibrating, I feel a sharp pain.
           |$\frac{1}{4}$ |$\frac{4}{4}$ A7 |
Come sit by me, don't say a word.
                | G D || D
Oh, can it be that I am slain!
                   | A7 |
Quick, Magdalena, take my gun.
                    | G D | D
Look, up in the hills, that flash of light!
         |$\frac{1}{4}$ |$\frac{4}{4}$ A7 |
Aim well, my little one,
                    | G D |$\frac{1}{4}$ D
We may not make it through the night.

       |$\frac{4}{4}$ A |
No llores, mi querida,
                  |
Dios nos vigila,
                     | G D |$\frac{1}{4}$ D
Soon the horse will take us to Durango.
    |$\frac{4}{4}$ A
Agárrame, mi vida,
                   |
Soon the desert will be gone.
              | G D ||
Soon you will be dancing the fandango.

Abandoned Love

WORDS AND MUSIC BY

BOB DYLAN

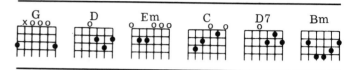

Moderately

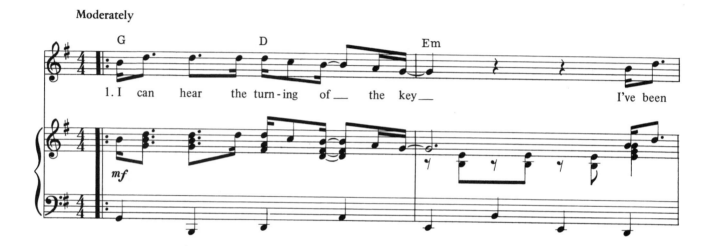

1. I can hear the turn-ing of __ the key __ I've been

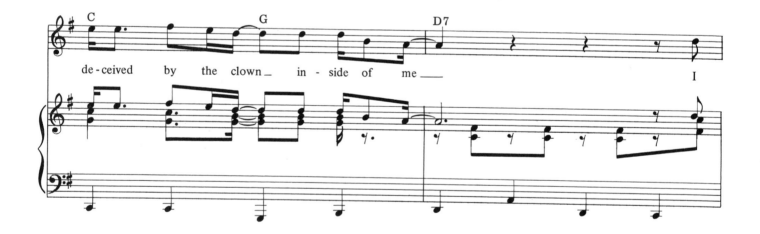

de-ceived by the clown __ in-side of me __ I

thought that he was right-eous but he's vain Oh,

some-thing's a-tell-ing me _____ I wear the ball and chain.

1.-7. 8.

2. My

2. My patron saint is a-fighting with a ghost
He's always off somewhere when I need him most
The Spanish moon is rising on the hill
But my heart is a-tellin' me
I love ya still

```
||G          D          |Em
 |C          G          |D7
|Bm                      |C
   |G        Bm C    |D7
     C  |G      |
```

3. I come back to the town from the flaming moon
I see you in the streets, I begin to swoon
I love to see you dress before the mirror
Won't you let me in your room one time
'Fore I finally disappear

```
||G          D          |Em
|C          G   |D7
|Bm                    |C
   |G         Bm    C |D7
        C  |G      |  ||
```

4. Everybody's wearing a disguise
To hide what they've got left behind their eyes
But me, I can't cover what I am
Wherever the children go
I'll follow them

```
G          D       |Em
  |C          G           |D7
  |Bm             |C
  |G    Bm  C |D7
        C  |G      |
```

5. I march in the parade of liberty
But as long as I love you I'm not free
How long must I suffer such abuse
Won't you let me see you smile one time
Before I turn you loose

```
||G          D          |Em
   |C          G          |D7
|Bm                    |C
      |G      BmC  |D7
        C  |G      |
```

6. I've given up the game, I've got to leave
The pot of gold is only make believe
The treasure can't be found by men who search
Whose gods are dead and whose queens
Are in the church

```
||G          D          |Em
   |C          G          |D7
 |Bm                          |C
    |G      Bm    C   |D7
        C  |G      |
```

7. We sat in an empty theater and we kissed
I asked ya please to cross me offa your list
My head tells me it's time to make a change
But my heart is telling me
I love ya but you're strange

```
G          D          |Em
|C          G          |D7
 |Bm                  |C
     |G    Bm  C  |D7
         C  |G      |   ||
```

8. One more time at midnight, near the wall
Take off your heavy make-up and your shawl
Won't you descend from the throne, from where you sit
Let me feel your love one more time
Before I abandon it

```
     G          D          |Em     |
     C          G          |D7
      |Bm                        |C
     |G    Bm  C   |D7
        C  |G      |   ||
```

Catfish

WORDS BY BOB DYLAN AND JACQUES LEVY
MUSIC BY BOB DYLAN

2. || Gm | G7 |
    Used to work on Mr. Finley's farm
    Gm | G7
    But the old man wouldn't pay
    | Gm | G7
    So he packed his glove and took his arm
    | Gm | G7
    An' one day he just ran away

    Db7 | C7 |
    Catfish
                | G7 | G7
    Million dollar man
    Eb7 | D7
    Nobody can throw the ball |
    C7
    Like Catfish can | G7 | ||

3. Gm | G7 |
    Come up where the Yankees are
    Gm | G7 |
    Dress up in a pin-stripe suit
    Gm | G7
    Smoke a custom-made cigar
    Gm | G7
    Wear an alligator boot

    Db7 | C7 |
    Catfish
                | G7 | G7
    Million dollar man
    Eb7 | D7
    Nobody can throw the ball |
    C7
    Like Catfish can | G7 | · ||

4. Gm | G7 |
    Carolina born and bred
    Gm | G7 |
    Love to hunt the little quail
    Gm | G7 |
    Got a hundred-acre spread
    Gm | G7
    Got some huntin' dogs for sale

    Db7 | C7 |
    Catfish
                | G7 | G7
    Million dollar man
    Eb7 | D7
    Nobody can throw the ball |
    C7 | G7 | ||
    Like Catfish can

5. Gm | G7 |
    Reggie Jackson at the plate
    Gm | G7 |
    Seein' nothin' but the curve
    Gm | G7 |
    Swing too early or too late
    Gm | G7
    Got to eat what Catfish serve

    Db7 | C7 |
    Catfish
                | G7 | G7
    Million dollar man
    Eb7 | D7
    Nobody can throw the ball |
    C7 | G7 | ||
    Like Catfish can

6. Gm | G7 |
    Even Billy Martin grins
    Gm | G7 |
    When the Fish is in the game
    Gm | G7 |
    Every season twenty wins
    Gm | G7
    Gonna make the Hall of Fame

    Db7 | C7 |
    Catfish
                | G7 | G7
    Million dollar man
    Eb7 | D7
    Nobody can throw the ball |
    C7 | G7 | G7   G9 ||
    Like Catfish can

Money Blues

WORDS BY BOB DYLAN AND JACQUES LEVY
MUSIC BY BOB DYLAN

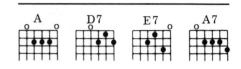

give it to my wom-an _____ She ain't got it no

more. _

2. A
   Went out last night

   Bought two eggs and a slice of ham
   D7
   Went out last night

   Bought two eggs and a slice of ham
   | E7
   Bill came to three dollars and ten cents
   | A | ||
   And I didn't even get no jam

3. A
   Man came around

   Askin' for the rent
   D7
   Man came around

   | A |
   Askin' for the rent
   | E7
   Well, I looked into the drawer
   | A | ||
   But the money's all been spent

4. A
   Well, well

   Ain't got no bank account
   D7
   Well, well

   | A | |
   Ain't got no bank account
   E7
   Went down to start one
   | A | ||
   But I didn't have the right amount

5. A
   Everything's inflated

   Like a tire on a car
   D7
   Everything's inflated

   | A |
   Like a tire on a car
   | E7
   Well, the man came and took my Chevy back
   | A | ||
   I'm glad I hid my old guitar

6. A
   Come to me, mama

   Ease my money crisis now
   D7
   Come to me, mama

   | A |
   Ease my money crisis now
   | E7
   I need something to support me
   | A | A A7 ||
   And only you know how

Rita May

WORDS BY **BOB DYLAN** AND **JACQUES LEVY**
MUSIC BY **BOB DYLAN**

Moderate Rock

Ri - ta May, Ri - ta May / You got your bod - y in the way.
May / How'd you ev - er get that way?
May / Lay - ing in a stack of hay.

You're so damn ___ non - cha - lant / But it's your mind that I want.
When do you ev - er see the light? / Don't you ev - er feel a fright?
Do you re - mem - ber where you been? / What's that cra - zy place you're in?

You got me huff - in' and a - puff - in' Next to you I feel like noth - in' Ri - ta
You got me burn - in' and I'm turn - in' But I know I must be learn - in' Ri - ta
I'm gon - na have to go to col - lege 'Cause you are the book of know - ledge Ri - ta

Sara

WORDS AND MUSIC BY

BOB DYLAN

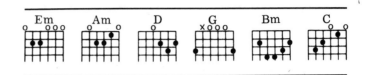

Moderately

1. I laid on a dune — I looked at the sky When the

chil-dren were ba-bies And played on the beach You

came up be-hind me I saw you go by You were

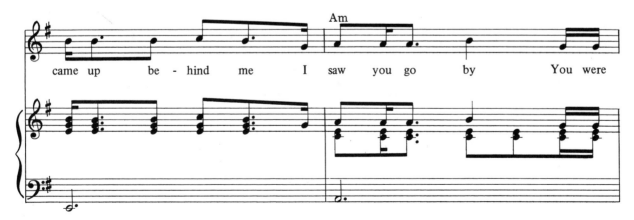

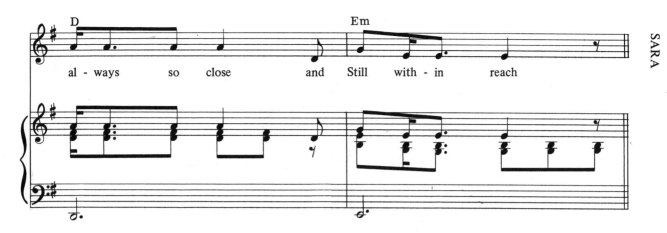

al - ways   so   close   and   Still   with - in   reach

Sa - ra, _____ Sa - ra

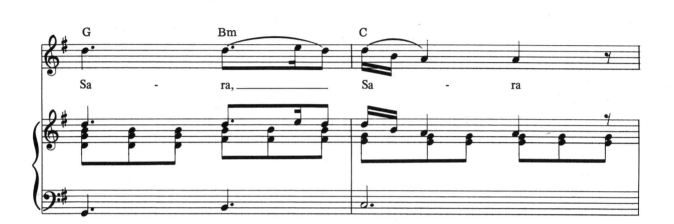

What - ev - er   made   you   want   to   change   your   mind

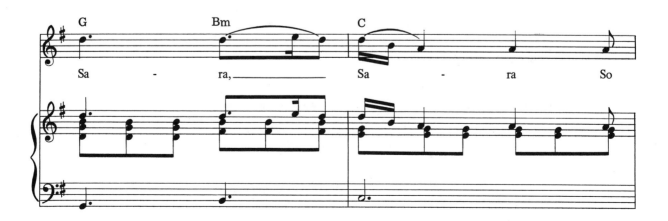

Sa - ra, _____ Sa - ra   So

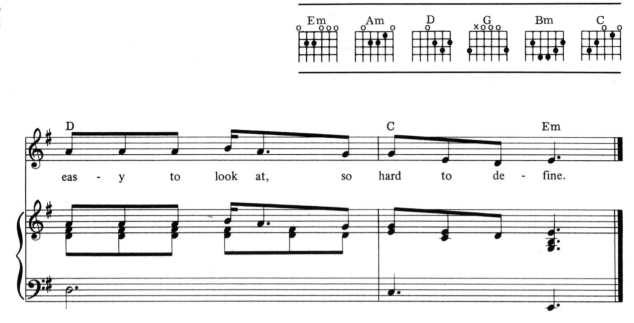

eas - y   to   look   at,   so   hard   to   de - fine.

2. ‖ Em
I can still see them playin'
| Am
With their pails in the sand
| D
They run to the water
| Em
Their buckets to fill
|
I can still see the shells
| Am
Fallin' out of their hands
| D   ‖
As they follow each other
Em   ‖
Back up the hill

G Bm | C |
Sara, Sara
D | C   Em |
Sweet virgin angel, sweet love of my life
G Bm | C |
Sara, Sara
D | C   Em   ‖
Radiant jewel, mystical wife

3. Em
Sleepin' in the woods
| Am |
By a fire in the night
D
Drinkin' white rum
| Em |
In a Portugal bar

Them playin' leap-frog
| Am |
And hearin' about Snow White
D
You in the market place
| Em   ‖
In Savanna-la-Mar

G Bm | C
Sara, Sara
| D | C   Em |
It's all so clear, I could never forget
G Bm | C
Sara, Sara
D | C   Em
Lovin' you is the one thing I'll never regret

4. ‖ Em
I can still hear the sounds
| Am
Of those Methodist bells
| D
I'd taken the cure
| Em |
And had just gotten through

Stayin' up for days
| Am
In the Chelsea Hotel
| D
Writin' "Sad-Eyed Lady
| Em   ‖
Of the Lowlands" for you

G Bm | C
Sara, Sara
| D | C   Em |
Wherever we travel we're never apart
G Bm | C
Sara, oh Sara
D | C   Em   ‖
Beautiful lady, so dear to my heart

5. Em |
How did I meet you
Am
I don't know
| D
A messenger sent me
| Em
In a tropical storm
|
You were there in the winter
| Am
Moonlight on the snow
| D
And on Lily Pond Lane
| Em   ‖
When the weather was warm

G Bm | C |
Sara, oh Sara
D | C   Em |
Scorpio Sphinx in a calico dress
G Bm | C
Sara, Sara
| D | C   Em
You must forgive me my unworthiness

6. ‖ Em
Now the beach is deserted
| Am
Except for some kelp
| D
And a piece of an old ship
| Em
That lies on the shore
|
You always responded
| Am
When I needed your help
| D
You gimme a map
| Em   ‖
And a key to your door

G Bm | C |
Sara, oh Sara
D | C   Em |
Glamorous nymph with an arrow and bow
G Bm | C
Sara, oh Sara
D | C   Em ‖
Don't ever leave me, don't ever go

Index of Titles, First Lines, and Key Lines

A NOTE ABOUT THIS BOOK

Music set by Music Art, Inc., New York City;
display typography by Royal Composing Room, New York City;
color printing for covers and slipcases by The Lehigh Press, Pennsauken, New Jersey;
text printing by The Murray Printing Company, Forge Village, Massachusetts;
mechanical binding by Sloves, New York City.

Book design and complete production by Helen Barrow.
Slipcase and binding design by Lidia Ferrara.
Slipcase and binding photograph by Paul Till.